INTERNATIONAL STUDIES QUARTERLY

Official Publication of the International Studies Association
Volume 25, Number 3, September 1981

CONTENTS

THE INTERNATIONAL STUDIES ASSOCIATION is a multidisciplinary organization which promotes interaction and collaboration among specialists whose interests are focused upon transnational phenomena. It seeks to develop an interdisciplinary capability for analyzing problems that cannot fruitfully be examined from the perspective of a single discipline. ISA also seeks to foster the growth of an international community of scholars, to encourage research of a problem-oriented nature (including both theoretical and policy concerns), to develop channels of communication between academicians and policy makers, and to improve the teaching of international studies.

MEMBERSHIP IN THE INTERNATIONAL STUDIES ASSOCIATION includes a subscription to the **QUARTERLY**, the ISA Newsletter, and other publications occasionally available for distribution to members. For information on regular and student membership fees, write to: Executive Office, International Studies Association, University of South Carolina, Columbia, South Carolina 29208. Members are advised to contact the ISA Executive Office regarding address changes and claims for undelivered publications.

Address correspondence about SUBMISSIONS to Editors, **INTERNATIONAL STUDIES QUARTERLY**, Harold Scott Quigley Center of International Studies, 1246 Social Sciences Building, University of Minnesota, Minneapolis, Minnesota 55455. Please submit FOUR COPIES of the manuscript, which should be typed, double-spaced, on one side of standard letter-size paper, and accompanied by a 300-word abstract. Footnotes and bibliographic citations should follow the current journal style or that shown in a style sheet available from the Editor or from the publisher, Sage Publications, Inc., 275 South Beverly Drive, Beverly Hills, California 90212. Since manuscripts are sent out for anonymous editorial evaluation, the author's name and affiliation should appear only on a separate cover page. Submission of a manuscript to ISQ implies that the work is not being considered for publication elsewhere. Submitted manuscript cannot be returned to authors.

INTERNATIONAL STUDIES QUARTERLY is published four times annually—in March, June, September, and December. Copyright © 1981 by the International Studies Association. All rights reserved. No portion of the contents may be reproduced in any form without written permission of the publisher, editor, and author(s).

Subscriptions: Regular institutional rate $46.00 per year; professionals, teachers, and students may obtain this **QUARTERLY** only through membership in the Association (see above). Add $2.00 for subscriptions outside the United States. Orders from the U.K., Europe, the Middle East, and Africa should be sent to London address (below). Orders from India should be sent to the New Delhi address (below).

Second class postage paid at Beverly Hills, California. ISSN 0020-8833

This journal is abstracted or indexed in **Human Resources Abstracts, International Political Science Abstracts, Historical Abstracts, Peace Research Reviews, Sage Urban Studies Abstracts, Public Affairs Information Service, Social Sciences Citation Index, Current Contents, Social Sciences Index, United States Political Science Documents,** and **ABC POL SCI,** and is available on microfilm from University Microfilms.

Back Issues: International Studies Quarterly was formerly published under the titles of: **Background on World Politics** (Volumes 1-5) and **Background: Journal of the International Studies Association** (Volumes 6-10). All volumes published are available on microfilm. For microfilm service and for replacement copies of **Background on World Politics** (Volumes 1-5), address inquiries directly to University Microfilms Library Services, Ann Arbor, Michigan 48106. Information about availability and prices of more recent back issues may be obtained from the publisher's order department (address below). Single-issue orders for 10 copies or more will receive special 50 percent adoption discount. Write to London office for sterling prices.

Inquiries: Address all correspondence and permissions requests to SAGE PUBLICATIONS, Inc., 275 South Beverly Drive, Beverly Hills, California 90212. Inquiries and subscriptions from the U.K., Europe, the Middle East, and Africa should be sent to SAGE PUBLICATIONS Ltd, 28 Banner Street, London EC1Y 8QE, England. From India, write to SAGE INDIA, P.O. 3605, New Delhi 110 024 India. Other orders should be sent to the Beverly Hills office.

Advertising: Current rates and specifications may be obtained by writing to the Advertising Manager at the Beverly Hills office (address above).

Claims: Claims for undelivered copies must be made no later than three months following month of publication. The publisher will supply missing copies when losses have been sustained in transit and when the reserve stock will permit.

Change of Address: Six weeks' advance notice must be given when notifying of change of address. Please send old address label along with the new address to insure proper identification. Please specify name of journal. POSTMASTER: Send change of address to: Journal name, c/o 275 South Beverly Drive, Beverly Hills, CA 90212

Industrialization in the Periphery

The Evolving Global Division of Labor

JAMES A. CAPORASO

Graduate School of International Studies
University of Denver

The emergence of the modern semiperiphery, or new industrializing countries, involving the rapid industrialization of parts of the less developed world, has received much attention in the scholarly literature. However, this phenomenon has met with radically different interpretations. To some, this peripheral industrialization signals a new era in north-south relations and a break with the old international division of labor based on the exchange of primary and industrial goods. To others, this new development is interpreted in a more limited way. It is seen as limited in terms of the number of possible new entrants, the temporary nature of the projected "boom" period, and the nonautonomous nature of the peripheral growth process.

An earlier version of this essay was inappropriately titled "One, Two, Many Japans." Through this title, including the double *entendre* "Two, Many," I meant to suggest not only the historical parallel of the present newly industrializing countries (NICs) with Japan during an earlier period, but also the possible absorptive limits of the global economy to the increasing number of newly arrived industrial *parvenus*. The Japanese parallel struck me as dramatically appropriate. The Japanese economy, as its contemporary counterparts, followed an export-led path to industrial development; in doing so, it attempted to restructure its economy through a rapid reallocation of resources from the primary to the

AUTHOR'S NOTE: An earlier version of this article was delivered under the title of "One, Two, Many Japans: Industrialization on the Periphery and Its Effects on the Advanced, Capitalist Countries" at a conference sponsored by the National Science Foundation on "The Widening Gap," Ojai, California, November 14-18, 1979. A subse-

INTERNATIONAL STUDIES QUARTERLY, Vol. 25 No. 3, September 1981 347-384
© 1981 I.S.A.

manufacturing sector, a swift structural transformation from light manufacturing to heavy industry, and an equally swift movement from heavy industry to industries that are more intensive in knowledge and technology. Accompanying these important changes, the state was to play a central role in the economy.

After some reflection, however, I was convinced that this was the wrong way to proceed. The modern semiperiphery, that set of countries[1] which has only recently succeeded in industrializing substantial portions of its economies, is different in important ways from the Japanese experience. These countries are different not just in the obvious descriptive ways (their late arrival, open [or penetrated] economies, dependence on foreign capital, technology, and markets), but also, quite possibly, in terms of the very causal structure of the process of industrialization.

By rejecting a serious pursuit of the historical parallel, I do not mean to endorse the doctrine that history is a collection of unique facts. Between the opposed philosophies that history involves the production of singular novelties and the view which sees the past as homogeneous, continuous, and infinitely divisible (each historical moment like every other), between the caricatures that "everything is unique" and its antinomy that "there is nothing new under the sun," lies a compromise position. This position, elegantly defended by Gerschenkron (1962), argues that we should

quent version was presented at a European Consortium for Political Research Workshop on Western Responses to the New International Economic Order, under the title "Peripheral Industrialization and Its Effects on Advanced Capitalist Countries," Florence, Italy, March 25-30, 1980. I am grateful for the many helpful comments and criticisms of participants at both conferences, and especially those of Colin Lawson and Michael Stohl. I also want to express my appreciation to Behrouz Zare, who helped with the data collection and some of the analysis and who provided many insightful suggestions along the way. Finally, many participants at the University of Denver's Fortnightly Gathering on Development meetings provided valuable comments, especially John Grove, Barry Hughes, Bill Loehr, John McCamant and Peter Van Ness.

1. Criteria that can be used to define the semiperiphery include both attributes of countries, such as economic growth and industrial transformation, as well as relational qualities such as position in a global division of labor, supply of intermediate and consumption goals to the center. The countries included in the semiperiphery in this essay are: Argentina, Mexico, Republic of Korea, Singapore, Portugal, Brazil, Hong Kong, the Phillipines, and Spain. The OECD labels this category the "newly industrializing countries" and focuses heavily on the attributes rather than relations in identifying countries. They have a slightly different list (OECD, 1979).

approach the question of industrial growth with developed theoretical positions but that we should be prepared to "see," and eventually to incorporate, new factors into our explanatory models. Instead of leaving the question of novelty on the metaphysical plane, Gerschenkron transforms it into a question of deviation from specified models. The identification of such deviations themselves become important puzzles, or anomalies, spurring us, we hope, toward theoretical refinements.

This article takes as its starting point an incontestable, but poorly understood, empirical observation, namely, that a small but significant group of less developed countries (LDCs) has grown dramatically in the last two decades, at least in economic terms. This growth pattern includes both general (overall) increases in national output (gross domestic product), even more rapid rates of industrial growth and, following logically from these differential growth rates, a rising share of manufactures in the total output of these countries. From 1960 to 1974, the LDCs as a group moved from a situation where 19 percent of their total exports were manufactures to one where manufactures accounted for 37% (Morton and Tulloch, 1977: 39). While this rapid growth and altered composition of output took place for LDCs as a whole, both trends were even more dramatic for the subgroup of NICs.

The primary task is to devise explanations of these new patterns of peripheral industrialization. To begin with, where does one go for insights, for productive ways of phrasing questions, for sources of conceptual leverage? Neoclassical economics provides one obvious body of knowledge. One way that neoclassical theory can approach the questions associated with peripheral industrialization is to call forth its stock of factors associated with economic growth and to ask, with particular reference to the countries in question, what is new with respect to these explanatory factors. Is there any significant change in the level of savings, investment, employed technologies, size or skill level of the labor force, and so on? In short, neoclassical theory is inclined to interpret this "new" phenomenon in terms of productive factors, shifting comparative advantages, and technical breakthroughs in the organization of production.

To anticipate portions of the remainder of this article, I feel that much progress can be made in understanding the phenomena associated with peripheral industrialization through application of neoclassical thought. There is an important sense in which capitalism has been "set loose" among the newly industrializing countries and it is precisely in this type of setting where neoclassical economics can make its greatest contribution.

However, I would expect neoclassical theory to have two weaknesses or blind spots. The first weakness centers on a series of questions having to do with the distributional, social, and political consequences of peripheral industrialization. What effects will rapid industrial growth have on the distribution of economic benefits, the positions of various classes and occupational groupings, and the role the state will play in economic planning and redistribution? In short, the expectation is that neoclassical thought will perform best when it isolates a system of economic variables from the rest of the social system and treats these variables as if they interacted in a closed system.

The second expected weakness can be stated succinctly. My suspicion is that neoclassical theory can provide an adequate account of what is going on once there is movement (that is, variation) in the variables central to its theoretical concerns. One could hardly expect otherwise of any theory. The peculiar difficulty arising in this context is that neoclassical arguments have a rather short historical reach; that is, they do not extend backward in time very far. I want to argue that, while there is nothing inherently defective about such arguments, they are forced to define as "extraneous" many important variables affecting their theories. Thus, to take one example, changes in the relations between capital and labor within the advanced, capitalist societies, or changes in the organization of capital itself, can have important consequences for LDCs in terms of the amount of capital exported to them. Once this capital is in the export realm, it enters the neoclassical equations. However, there is no attempt to reach backward (historically) and to incorporate these remote conditions into the overall theory. As a result, a sense of history, of process, is missed.

Theories drawn from the academic left, of the Marxian and dependencia variety, also offer their mixtures of insights and limitations. On the positive side, these theories almost uniformly join a focus on the external global system (in particular its sources of capital, markets, technology, and military force) with analysis of the distributional issues within the peripheral developing country. Since the theoretical starting point of Marxism is the law of unequal development, scholars within this tradition are encouraged to examine the effect of external ties on sectoral inequalities, class inequalities, and regional inequalities.

Another attractive general feature of the Marxian approach is that it encourages us to look further back in time, from proximal causes to more remote ones. This has the effect not only of placing our knowledge on a firmer historical foundation, but also facilitates an understanding of just how episodic or enduring will be such things as capital export, multinational corporate expansion, and liberal access to markets. If these variables are taken as exogenous, as given, then there is no way (by definition) to account for their change, despite the very real possibility that the direction and magnitude of their movements shape the opportunities and limits of peripheral development. By "expanding backward" in time, the Marxian approach becomes a contender at least for a proper theoretical understanding of the temporal nature of contemporary peripheral capitalist development.

The above account is a vast simplification, of course. There are large disagreements within Marxian and dependencia theories as to the benefits of dependent development (that is, development which relies extensively on the global capitalist system) to the peripheral country as a whole. Indeed, the strong focus on distributional issues in both bodies of thought does not facilitate an exploration of the issue of the welfare consequences of peripheral development for the country as a whole. In fairness to these traditions, "the whole country" is not seen as a very meaningful unit of analysis.

A second limitation is less understandable from the standpoint of Marxian and dependency theory. In neither body of thought is there an adequate dynamic account of the relationship between economic growth and equity. Marx himself saw the process of growth as an exploitative one, with some growing richer as a result of the surplus appropriation of the value created by others. Marxian scholars since then have updated Marx's distributional analysis by analyzing how the state plays a role in modifying the economic dynamics proposed by Marx. Whether one interprets the distributive role of the state in a positive way, as one of creating equity out of market-generated abundance, or in a more negative way, as a spinoff of its demand-management and consumption policies, makes little difference here. My argument is that a sustained theoretical account of the economic growth-social equity nexus is not provided in many studies of peripheral growth. This is particularly a blind spot for dependency theory which, since it identifies the sources of inequality in commercial relations among countries (rather than in production relations), cannot even produce a determinate analytic account of domestic inequality.

My task in this article will be to examine a number of countries which have expanded their industrial sectors in the last twenty years, to attempt to identify the broad sources of this important change, and to consider together national and international factors. The remainder of this essay comes in four parts. First, I will address the question of the utility of the semiperiphery (or newly industrializing countries) as a category of analysis. Second, I will briefly outline the methods to be used. Third, I will present some purely descriptive data on the major aspects of change in the semiperiphery. Fourth, I will examine some of the sources of these changes. I will not, as originally planned, speak to the issue of the dangers and limitations that the semiperiphery takes on by its involvement in the international capitalist system. While such an analysis is important, and in my mind the costs and benefits are not well established, there is simply not enough space to adequately confront this complex set of issues here.[2]

2. In the earlier version of this essay presented at Ojai, California, I suggested that the dangers included: protectionist responses from the advanced, capitalist countries; external penetration and control; fragmentation of the LDCs; concentration of LDC interactions on a few suppliers and markets; and the difficulty of moving the economy in a more diversified direction. Since this earlier version, it has become clear to me that at least three

The Capitalist Semiperiphery
As a Category of Analysis

Twenty years ago, the term "Third World" conveyed some descriptive information about countries which were not part of either the advanced capitalist world or the socialist world. Today, the "Third World" has become a more complicated place. To be sure, these countries still have, on the average, more acute poverty than the countries in the OECD or Council of Mutual Economic Assistance (COMECON),[3] lower quality of life, and lower life expectancies. However, as the value of a category diminishes with the heterogeneity of its components, it has become difficult to use the term Third World without constant qualification.

There are many examples of this emerging variety. Brazil, with its dynamic economy and huge (and growing) manufacturing center is one case in point. India, with its large steel industry, is another. In addition to the "Brazilian model," there are the small, Asian "late-developers," "those other Japans" (or Asian Hollands) as some have called them. These countries who specialize in labor-intensive industries where technologies are relatively standardized, hence mobile, include South Korea, Taiwan, Hong Kong, and Singapore.

This new pattern of industrialization is not limited to areas we normally think of as undeveloped. The semi-industrialized but rapidly growing southern periphery of Europe in which Spain, Portugal, Greece, Turkey, and Yugoslavia are included is a case in point. So the group is quite varied, consisting of large countries with generous endowments of natural resources, small countries from Asia, and older countries on the southern periphery of Europe.

---

other concerns must be added to this already formidable agenda: the problem of debt and foreign exchange crises; the complex question of the kinds of political structures and policies that often accompany (and are needed in?) late, dependent, industrializing countries; and, the limits on the number of new entrants into the capitalist semiperiphery. Is the global division of labor an elastic one, capable of accommodating a large (and flexible) number of entrants, or is it more inelastic, and once a certain number has been admitted, it closes up? Difficult questions to be sure, and ones that require sustained analysis.

3. The members of COMECON are Bulgaria, Cuba, Czechoslovakia, German Democratic Republic, Hungary, Mongolia, Poland, Romania, and the Union of Soviet Socialist Republics. Finland and Yugoslavia are associate members.

I see three advantages in focusing on the countries in the semiperiphery. The first advantage is that by observing countries within this category, our attention focuses on those processes within the less developed world (as well as between them and the advanced capitalist countries) where there is the most movement, or change. This change, dramatized and thrown into relief by the relative stagnation of the remaining LDCs,[4] provides a clear and interpretable series of cases where economic growth and diversification did occur and continue to occur.

A second reason for studying the semiperiphery is that most of these countries follow the capitalist path to economic growth, and it is hoped, to development. A focus on these countries might allow us to assess the effectiveness and limitations of this strategy while at the same time providing an opportunity to see the operation of peripheral capitalism in its most advanced form. As Peter Evans (1979: 9) put it:

> A number of larger and richer countries no longer stand at the edge of the international division of labor, exporting primary products to the center and receiving manufactured goods in return. . . . These Third World countries now have within their borders an increasingly diversified industrial capacity. At the same time, the penetration of international capital into their social and economic life is increasingly thorough.

By focusing on capitalism in the periphery we do not have to confine our interest to less developed countries. This is because peripheral capitalism is not an isolated capitalism or more fully, it is not a self-contained, autonomous capitalism. Instead, peripheral capitalism integrates the capitalism of the center with that of the periphery. One theme which I will try to develop later is that it is impossible to understand the emergent changes in the periphery without taking into account changes in the organization of capital, in labor-capital relations, and in the relations between capital and the state within the advanced countries.

A third reason for studying the semiperiphery is that such a focus raises a series of interesting, if frustrating, questions. Why is

4. In an absolute sense, that is, compared to their own past performance, the LDCs are certainly not stagnating.

this group of countries moving so rapidly into the manufacturing areas? What role do foreign capital and technology play in this transition? What role do economic factors within the advanced capitalist countries (ACCs) play and, in turn, what are the probable effects of peripheral growth on the ACCs? What are the possibilities and limits of this type of industrialization? Can it go on indefinitely, or are there ceiling effects? Are there structural limitations to the accommodation of further entrants into the semiperiphery? What will happen if and when new actors embark on this path to industrialization? Will the current South Koreas and Brazils be bumped upward, downward, sideward, or not bumped at all? Finally, what are the implications of this type of industrial growth for the forms of state power most likely to emerge in these countries?

METHODS AND PROCEDURES

For my purposes in this article, I have decided to use three criteria to identify countries in the semiperiphery: overall growth rate from 1960 to 1975, growth rate of the manufacturing sector, and the share of manufactures over total gross domestic product. While each of these criteria is thought of as a continuous scale, I decided on a minimum requirement of 19% for the third indicator, share of manufactures over GDP. This is to rule out inclusion of countries that have rapid growth rates on a very small base. Using these three criteria, I have come up with the following list of countries: Argentina, Mexico, South Korea, Singapore, Portugal, Brazil, Hong Kong, the Philippines, and Spain.

Descriptive Data on
Semiperipheral Countries

For the first fifteen to twenty years after World War II, economic growth and trade involvement of the LDCs increased very slowly. Indeed, until the mid-1960s, the LDCs had a steadily declining share of world exports (Chenery and Keesing, 1979: 1). However, since the mid-1960s, this situation has changed dramatically, with LDCs as a whole and the semiperipheral countries in particular gaining in shares of world industrial production and world industrial exports. From 1965 to 1974, the LDCs as a group expanded their manufacturing exports to developed countries by a real growth rate of 16.1% per year (Keesing, 1979: 18). This rate of expansion is large and outpaces that for any other grouping of countries with the possible exception of the socialist countries in Eastern Europe. These changes signalled the potential for a substantial reallocation of industrial and commercial activity (Chenery, 1979: 457).

There are several trends that I will briefly explore in this section: overall economic growth of the semiperiphery; manufacturing growth, manufacturing exports; and export concentration.

Overall Economic Growth. In Table 1 are the data on annual growth rates for our selected countries.

These figures show that the economies of the countries were performing in a consistently strong manner from 1960 to 1974. The annual average growth rates were high, though these ranged considerably, from a low of 4.6% in Argentina to a high of 9.6% in the Republic of Korea. For comparison purposes, the annual average growth rate for advanced capitalist countries for the same period was 4.7% and for North America 3.9%. Of course, members of the less developed world were, by definition, starting from a much lower base, but this alone counts for very little, since the countries in the poorest categories have not been able to industrialize or to grow rapidly in the primary sector.

Manufacturing Growth. If we turn toward Table 2, we see that the rates of growth for the manufacturing sector are even more dramatic. The annual average growth rate for the Republic of Korea, from 1960 to 1974, was 18.5%, for Singapore 13.7%, and for Brazil 8%. Again, as a reference for comparison, advanced capitalist countries had an annual average growth rate of 5.9 % from 1960 to 1974, the European Community grew at a rate of 5.4%, and North America at the rate of 4.9% (United Nations, 1976).

Although the differences between growth rates of these various groupings are pronounced, one might also point out that large

TABLE 1
Annual Rates of Growth at Constant Prices (in percentage GDP)

	1961	1962	1963	1964	1965	1966	1967	1968	1969	1970	1971	1972	1973	1974	1960-1974
Argentina	7.1	-1.6	-2.4	10.3	9.2	0.6	2.6	4.4	8.5	5.4	4.8	3.1	6.1	6.5	4.6
Mexico	4.9	4.7	8.0	11.7	6.5	6.9	6.3	8.1	6.3	6.9	3.4	7.3	7.6	5.9	6.9
Korea (Republic of)	5.1	3.0	8.8	8.6	6.0	12.0	7.3	12.8	15.2	8.6	9.8	7.3	16.9	8.7	9.6
Singapore	8.4	7.0	10.0	-3.5	7.5	11.1	11.8	13.9	13.7	-1.7	12.5	13.4	11.5	6.3	8.8
Portugal	5.5	6.7	5.9	6.6	7.5	4.1	7.5	9.7	2.1	7.8	5.7	8.7	11.0	4.3	6.6
Brazil	10.5	4.6	1.3	4.0	2.8	4.7	4.6	9.0	9.6	*	*	*	*	*	4.8
Hong Kong	*	10.2	10.3	9.1	18.1	6.6	8.6	3.7	14.2	6.2	3.1	7.3	12.6	-0.0	8.5
Philippines	5.4	5.0	6.8	3.1	5.2	4.9	6.1	5.6	5.3	6.0	5.9	4.7	9.2	*	5.5
Spain	11.8	9.3	8.8	6.2	7.2	8.3	4.3	5.7	7.8	6.0	4.3	9.6	7.4	5.4	6.9

SOURCE: *National Account Statistics*. New York: United Nations, 1976.
NOTE: Data in each column represent the growth rate for that year and the preceding year. Data in last column represent the average, annual growth rate for all years.
*Data not available.

TABLE 2
Annual Rates of Growth in Manufacturing at Constant Prices (in percentages)

	1961	1962	1963	1964	1965	1966	1967	1968	1969	1970	1971	1972	1973	1974	1960-1974
Argentina	10.0	-5.5	-4.1	18.9	13.8	0.7	1.5	6.9	10.4	6.3	9.7	6.0	6.4	6.8	6.3
Mexico	5.5	4.6	9.2	17.4	9.5	9.4	6.8	10.1	8.1	8.7	3.1	8.3	8.9	7.4	8.6
Philippines	3.4	5.1	6.8	2.9	4.4	6.5	9.3	6.9	5.3	6.2	7.6	6.0	11.3	4.1	6.3
Singapore	5.8	8.5	16.8	3.7	13.4	14.3	20.1	20.7	22.5	-1.9	18.7	16.8	16.3	3.8	13.7
Portugal	6.6	6.4	7.0	15.2	10.2	6.9	7.6	12.5	5.9	9.4	7.9	12.4	14.6	2.6	9.2
Brazil	6.6	6.2	5.8	5.1	-4.7	12.3	2.4	15.9	10.8	11.0	11.3	14.1	15.8	*	8.0
Hong Kong	*	*	*	*	*	*	*	*	*	*	*	*	*	*	*
Korea (Republic of)	3.1	13.2	17.3	6.5	20.0	17.1	22.8	27.0	21.4	18.4	17.7	15.7	30.9	17.5	18.5
Spain	*	*	*	*	*	*	*	*	*	*	*	*	*	*	*

SOURCE: *National Account Statistics*. New York: United Nations, 1976.
NOTE: Data in each column represent the growth rate for that year and the preceding year. Data in last column represent the average, annual growth rate for all years.
*Data not available.

TABLE 3
Comparison Between Two Groups of Semiperipheral Countries (1975)

	Exports/GDP	Manufactured Exports/Total Exports
I		
Argentina	6.1	22.2
Brazil	7.0	25.6
Mexico	4.5*	48.2
II		
Portugal	13.1	70.0
Singapore	95.3	41.8
South Korea	25.0	81.5
Taiwan	26.1**	76.4**
Hong Kong	62.9	96.9

SOURCE: *Commodity Trade Statistics, National Account Statistics*, various issues.
*Data for 1974.
**Data for 1970.

differences exist within the semiperiphery. The growth rate of South Korea (18.5%) is almost three times that of Argentina (6.3%) and the Phillipines (6.3%). Similarly, as Table 3 shows, the export orientation of the three Latin American countries is small by comparison with the Asian Mix and Portugal. In addition, there is a close correlation between reliance on exports and the share of manufactures in total exports. Argentina, Brazil, and Mexico are large countries with sizable internal markets and plentiful natural resources. Perhaps the rate of growth in such countries is dictated more by the tempo of internal demand rather than the cyclical ebbs and flows of the international economy.

Manufacturing Exports. The level of manufactured exports and the growth rates for newly industrializing countries raise important questions, particularly since many scholars argue that manufactured exports are the engines of growth behind the more general process of peripheral industrialization. In this light, it is interesting to see that manufactured exports increased at a rate of over 12% a year from 1960 to 1975 (Chenery and Keesing, 1979: 12). A large share of these exports originated in the semiperipheral countries we are dealing with here. As Chenery and Keesing show (1979: 13), South Korea, Spain, Hong Kong, and Taiwan together supply 45% of the total.

Along with this increase in manufactured exports, LDCs in general, and semiperipheral countries in particular, have altered the composition of their exports. If fuels are excluded from LDC exports, we find that in 1960 manufactures accounted for 19% of exports and in 1974 the share rose to 42% (Morton and Tulloch, 1974: 42). For some of the semiperipheral countries the figures in 1975 were as follows: South Korea 82%; Taiwan 85%; Mexico 52%; Brazil 27%; Hong Kong 97%; Singapore 43%; and Spain 70% (OECD, 1979: 47).

This dramatic upswing in the export of manufactures has had an effect on world market shares for manufactured goods. For example, in 1963, the semiperipheral countries on our list (minus the Philippines) accounted for only 2% of the world exports of manufactures; by 1976, this figure had jumped to 5.24%.[5] The primary markets into which these countries moved were those traditionally supplied by members of the OECD. The share of the semiperiphery in OECD manufactured imports rose from 2.6% in 1963 to 8.1% in 1977 (OECD, 1979: 6). While the semiperiphery has made only a modest dent in terms of the global picture, it has made considerable strides over its own past behavior. Furthermore, the political impact of these countries' market shares may be much larger than the size of the share suggests, and may be more closely related to marginal changes over a period of time.

Concentration of Manufactured Exports Among Less Developed Countries. The newly industrializing countries were selected precisely because of their rapid expansion into manufacturing production and manufactured exports and, when we focus on them, their achievements cannot be denied.[6] However, when we shift our attention to the less developed world as a whole, the picture changes quite sharply.

As Morton and Tulloch point out (1977: 155-158), the exports of manufactures are not a significant source of export earnings for most LDCs. Out of 85 countries included in their analysis, slightly greater than one-half received less than 5% of their export proceeds from manufactures (Morton and Tulloch, 1977: 157). Indeed, out of the entire group, there were only 22 countries

5. These figures were calculated from OECD data (OECD, 1979: 19).

6. I do not mean to imply that rapid industrialization of the semiperiphery has no negative consequences for the industrializing countries, or for others. Clearly it does. However, the exact nature and degree of these negative consequences are themselves the subjects of complex investigations.

TABLE 4
Trends of Manufactured Exports by Region

Region	Percent Figures (1976 data estimated)		
	1965	1970	1976
East Asia	38	48	60
Latin America	14	16	17
Turkey and Yugoslavia	14	10	8
South Asia	22	15	8
Middle East and North Africa	7	7	5
Sub-Saharan Africa	5	4	2
Total	100	100	100

SOURCE: Keesing, 1979: 16.

which received 20% or more of their export earnings from manufactures.

Further, as Table 4 shows, there is an interregional concentration of manufactured exports. Strong interregional concentration is suggested by the fact that Asia accounts for over 50% of the manufactured exports, Latin America 17%, and Africa less than 10%. Within regions, we note that Hong Kong and South Korea account for the bulk of East Asian exports, India accounts for the greatest share in South Asia, and Mexico and Brazil are the largest exporters in Latin America. The production and export of manufactures by LDCs is not very widespread and is not clear from the countries which are currently industrializing that their inroads can be successfully imitated.

The Sources of
Peripheral Industrialization

In attempting to answer the question of the sources of peripheral industrialization, one is tempted to compile a long list of variables representing all the causal sources mentioned. This kind of approach is suggested by the literature, which often deals with one part of the total problem. For example, some scholars see country characteristics such as market size, income levels, and the abundance of human capital as being important (Chenery and Keesing, 1979) while others find the answer in the policies pursued by the state, such as export promotion, capital attraction, and certain fiscal and monetary policies. Still others see changes in systemic phenomena as important. The opportunities opened up by changes in the global division of labor, the movement away from resource-intensive and labor-intensive industries in the advanced capitalist countries, the improvements in transportation and communication facilitating both the movement of goods and the control of capital from abroad, have all encouraged the expansion of capital from center to periphery.

This is not the place to argue for the importance or nonimportance of any one factor or set of factors. My point is that all of these formulations, taken together, beg a very important question. How do all these separate factors add up? Here I am not thinking primarily of the relative weights of particular variables. This is an empirical question, to be solved by model estimation. The problems lie at another level. They involve questions of causal priority, temporal sequencing, redundancies in causal influence, substitution effects, and interaction effects. In short, these are questions related to the proper specification of the theory. The remainder of my essay will offer an argument about the sources of peripheral industrialization.

The Accumulation of Capital. There are many factors associated with peripheral industrialization but none, in my opinion, is so central as the process of capital accumulation. By capital accumulation,[7] I mean the process through which economic actors (individuals, firms, states) expand their productive capabilities (machinery, tools) over various cycles of the production-consumption process. This conceptualization brings our attention directly to the *rate* at which the expansion of capital takes place.

A theoretical understanding of this process is furthered by the concept of surplus, taken from Marxian economic theory. A country, or firm, cannot increase its productive output without

---

7. For discussions of this concept, the reader is referred to Marx (1906: ch. 23-25), Barratt-Brown (1974: ch. 3), and Becker (1977: chs. 2 and 8).

generating a surplus, withholding part of that surplus from consumption, and further directing part of that surplus into productive channels, that is, reinvesting part of it in new machinery, technology, new forms of work organization and so on. Doing the above increases either the scale and/or the quality of capital equipment, and hence increases output. This opens the possibility for larger surpluses, that is, larger amounts of money capital remaining after paying for replacement of capital equipment (that is, depreciation) and for wages. Even on the assumption that the ratio of the surplus to the wages paid to labor is the same, that is, on the assumption of constant shares for both, the absolute size of the surplus can grow, thus permitting a larger reinvestment in capital goods. However, if technological change results in the acquisition of capital goods that are "labor-saving," or even "de-skilling" in the sense of lowering requirements for operators of machinery, the share of wages in the wages-surplus pie will decrease.[8]

Here it is useful to stop and point to a special significance of this formulation for less developed societies, a significance that becomes most apparent through contrast with advanced capitalist societies. In these advanced societies, the process of capital accumulation depends not only on the productivity of capital but also on the share of output paid back to labor. This latter quantity is substantial. In many industrial sectors, labor is organized and its organization increases its bargaining power. Within countries of the periphery and semiperiphery, by contrast, labor is not well organized and is often not allowed to be. This provides a great potential for generating a large surplus and reinvesting such a surplus back into productive goods.

The point of production, from the standpoint of capital accumulation, is to produce not just for consumption but to have something left over and to use this quantity for productive purposes: not for money hoarding, building Gothic churches or pyramids, or storing wealth in concrete but unproductive possessions, such as art treasures, land, and so on.

8. In this latter case, where surplus increases faster than wages, Marxian theory speaks of the rate of exploitation of labor.

Let me try to summarize the argument thus far, relying on the following Marxist identity for expository purposes.

$c + v + s$ = total output
where: c = the cost of capital equipment
v = the costs of labor
s = the surplus

If c, the capital advanced, yields a product which can just pay for labor (v), plus the actual capital consumed in the process, plus a fund for the capitalist's consumption, there is nothing left over. The production relationship is reproduced but the quantity c is not expanded.

In Marxian terms, the above illustration satisfies the conditions for simple reproduction (Marx, 1906: 621). Capital perpetuates itself but does not expand, that is, does not accumulate. On the other hand, if there remains an additional part of the surplus after returning to workers and capitalists their respective consumption funds and replacing the consumed part of the capital originally advanced, and if this quantity is plowed back into capital equipment, then capital accumulation is taking place. Under these conditions, production under capitalism assumes its dynamic form, producing to sell, selling to realize a surplus, realizing a surplus to produce, now at a more advanced level than before. As Barratt Brown (1974: 53) put it, "It is the part of the S (surplus) that is reinvested that is necessary for the capitalist's survival."

Once we place capital accumulation at the center of the process of peripheral industrialization, other phenomena become interpretable in relation to it. The importance of links to the international economy, in the form of foreign direct investment and loans from international financial institutions, are seen as vehicles for building up a capital base. The strong role of the state can be seen not only as a fine-tuner of domestic demand but, perhaps more importantly, in its twin role as entrepreneur itself, and as a dampener of rising wage demands. Specific economic policies, such as generous credit and tax policies toward export-oriented industries, become interpretable not only in light of market-expanding intentions, but also as a way of directing scarce public resources toward industries with the highest capacity for generating a surplus. In short, many variables which were previously seen as independent of one another now assume a more coherent form.

In addition, identifying the central problem as one of accumulation perhaps provides us with some leverage in answering the question of why growth in the semiperiphery occurs in such rapid spurts, why it assumes, à la Gerschenkron (1962), the form of a "big push" rather than an incremental flow.

Along these lines, Gerschenkron argued for three possibilities, none of which is exclusive of the others as far as I can see. The first possibility is that there are certain indivisibilities on the supply side, or, in different words, that a minimum critical mass is required for certain inputs into the productive process. One could think of the "minimum capital needs of an industrializing economy" or the "minimum size of the individual industrial firm and the availability of technologically required inputs" (Gerschenkron, 1962: 35). These thoughts, formulated with late nineteenth/early twentieth century industrializing countries in mind, seem all the more insightful and relevant to me in the context of our present internationalized economies, in which domestic economic units must compete with larger foreign ones. Thus, the pressures toward uniformity of industry structure and behavior are heightened today by the internationalization of capital, production, and marketing.

On the demand side, Gerschenkron offers a similarly stimulating argument, namely that if industrialization is to occur at all, it must occur along a broad front. This is so because industrialization is a process which by its nature demands high levels of specialization. Enterprises emerge, and sustain their growth through mutual demand and exchange for each other's products (Gerschenkron, 1962: 35). I would add a qualification to this argument. Just as the supply side of the argument gathered momentum along with the increasing internationalization of domestic economies, the demand side loses momentum.

I would expect the factors on the demand side of the equation to lose momentum precisely because some of the factors that normally function as benefits on the input side of the equation (such as capital and technology for differentiated economic activities, availability of capital goods and so on) operate in a perverse way on the demand side. To put the problem simply, the domestic and international economy have become so enmeshed, and so differentiated, that ancillary economic activities once necessarily associated with the performance of an economic function inside the domestic economy now transpire outside. In short, what has been taking place over a long historical frame, but is accented in the last twenty years, is a progressive decoupling of economic functions from a single territorial base. Both upstream and downstream, toward raw material sources and markets, there is an unquestionable movement regarding an interchanging of economic activities. This is evidenced most forcefully in the logic of international subcontracting and part-processing, two phenomena which we will examine below. For now I only want to establish that complex series of economic activities, once geographically concentrated and explainable theoretically in terms of the laws of agglomeration in regional economics, are now organized in spatially more complex ways. As dependency theorists well know, parts of an economy may be highly developed and yet depend for their crucial inputs and output linkages on external actors (Brewster, 1973: 5; Sunkel, 1973).

The third possibility offered by Gerschenkron is complementary to the other two and can, in my opinion, act as a multiplier of the supply-side and demand-side arguments. Here Gerschenkron lays special importance on the rapid growth potential of "late industrializers." Two separate properties are given special importance: one, the extent to which industrialization has been delayed; two, the degree of backwardness in a country on the eve of its industrialization.

Why are these two factors important in explaining the big push? First, as Gerschenkron (1962: 44) explicitly argues, the more backward the country, the greater the tendency to have industrialization proceed under some organized direction (for example, banks, bureaucratic controls). This tendency gives to economic growth an uneven aspect that would not characterize a market-dominated process. Second, there is the extent to which industrial development is "delayed" or, more simply, "late." What is important is not so much "lateness per se," but rather the technological gap, as well as the labor cost gap more subtly, between the backward and most advanced countries.

The reasoning behind the hypothesis is twofold. The first part rests on a technological gap between the advanced countries and the less advanced ones, and the benefits that would accrue to the less advanced if the technology could be transferred and put to productive use in it. In a sense, the opportunity for rapid growth can be thought of as a function of the distance between the "ceiling" and the "floor," with asymptotically declining possibilities for growth as one approaches the upper limits. The ceiling could be thought of as a technological optimum, an optimal production possibility curve dependent on the best appropriate technology available on the world market. The "availability" qualification rules out high-level technologies controlled through patents and restrictive research and development policies but not the standardized technologies that can be purchased on the open market.

The second leg of this argument rests on a combination of two differentials: cost of labor and productivity differentials. The argument here is simply that, the lower the gap in productivity between two countries and the higher the difference in costs, the greater the flow of capital and accompanying technology from the higher cost to lower cost country. Given the fact that there are many standardized technologies which are guarded by neither investing states nor firms, and if we further consider that these technologies require a disciplined but not highly skilled labor force, it should not be surprising that output per worker and quality of product converge across labor pools in different countries (Landsberg, 1979: 57; U.S. Tariff Commission, 1970).

I have suggested that the process of accumulation is central. What is it that accounts for accumulation? There are many factors, but here I want to subsume them under four groups: pull factors, push factors, facilitating factors, and conversion factors. The pull and push factors can be thought of as properties more or less attached to the receiving and sending units, for example, the receiver and sender of capital and technology. The term "pull" is intended to convey the sense in which the LDC can attract or "pull in" resources from the external sector. Similarly, the term "push" is intended to convey the sense in which, more or less independently of the external attractions, there are forces repelling capital and technology from the advanced, capitalist countries. Facilitative factors are those that are not attached to specific countries at all and are therefore "available" to LDCs. They include factors in the public domain, such as certain parts of scientific knowledge, the levels of technology in transportation and communications or standardized technologies for production. Conversion factors refer simply to the ways in which decision makers (private and public) in the industrializing country utilize their internal and external resources, that is, how they convert these resources into outputs, one of which is economic development.

PULL FACTORS

There are well over one hundred less developed countries in today's world. Yet the nine we focus on here have set themselves apart in a marked way over the last twenty years. The most important question we can ask is why (that is, why these countries?) and the most natural place to start is by examining these countries themselves.[9]

The first fact to note about the semiperipheral countries themselves is that they have, on the whole, much larger markets than the other LDCs (Chenery and Keesing, 1979: 3-5; Chenery,

---

9. This decision of course may reflect a theoretical prejudice on my part, in particular that the nation-state is the primary causal unit, or at least organizer of those causal forces which affect industrialization and development. To those who see economic change as responding to the inexorable forces of global capitalism, operating both subnationally and transnationally, this decision may be quite "unnatural." At this point I simply ask the readers' patience and remind them that while I begin with the nation-state, I do not intend to end there.

1979b: 461-468). Even as far back as 1950, Mexico had a gross domestic product per capita of $475, Brazil's was $335, and Argentina's was $1027 (Chenery, 1979: 465-466). No doubt this factor did exert a pull on the advanced capitalist countries, a pull that was first manifest in the exports of goods to these markets and later transformed to the export of capital. Peter Evans (1979: 75) has provided striking evidence for this "follow-on" imperative, that is, for the tendency of capital exports in the form of foreign direct investment to replace the export of goods. He shows that the sectoral distribution of manufactured imports into Brazil in 1949 mirrors quite faithfully the sectoral distribution of foreign direct investment in manufactured goods in 1972, a fit that would be most improbable under the assumption of independence of investment and trade. What this evidence suggests is that foreign direct investment in the periphery may be, at least partly, a market-preservation strategy, an attempt to defend market shares in the face of increasing international and local competition.

Evans's findings and theoretical interpretation are not new of course. The general theoretical argument from which defensive investments can be deduced is the product cycle theory, a theory offered in coherent form by Raymond Vernon (1966, 1971). This theory suggests that a product has a natural cycle, from birth through growth, maturation, and decline. Vernon expected new products to originate in countries such as the United States, where both consumer tastes and the distribution of productive factors favored product innovation. In particular, the United States seemed to satisfy the conditions of capital abundance, labor scarcity (especially artisanal labor), and consumption patterns that went well beyond human necessities. Once the product is established, the salience of the original productive factors diminishes and strategies of mass production and commercialization take over. Here the costs of labor and those of capital assume greater importance. Further, because of the worldwide sourcing of capital by MNCs, this factor assumes less importance than the cost of labor.

The innovation phase is then followed by production for the domestic mass market and export abroad. But as the product matures, other firms in other countries acquire the technology and compete with the innovator in both foreign and home markets. As a response to these trends, the innovating firm now exports its capital to foreign countries to take advantage of the cheap labor costs and ready access to local markets.

A focus on the dynamic properties of the product cycle leads us to the second pull factor, the pools of abundant and cheap labor in these countries. Here the prime stimulus is not a market for finished goods but the cost-cutting advantages deriving from access to a cheap productive factor. While the productivity differentials between advanced, capitalist countries and the semiperiphery are quite small in many traditional manufacturing sectors, the labor cost differences are huge. Landsberg (1979: 57-58), using data from the U.S. Tariff Commission, reports that the "net Far East labor cost for electronic assembly works out to be only eight percent of that in the U.S." With wages and benefits low, productivity approaching U.S. levels, restrictions concerning safety and pollution weak, foreign capital finds an attractive niche in which to operate.

The attraction of cheap labor builds on a related pull factor, the existence of export platforms and free production zones within certain third world countries (Fröbel et al., 1978; Robinson, 1979; Stohl and Targ, forthcoming). These industrial enclaves provide attractive locations for labor-intensive, industrial processing within LDCs and the easy export of these goods to worldwide markets. What these free production zones offer are low taxes, generous credit, cheap labor, and a minimum of government interference. These export platforms are especially useful when the advantages of mechanized forms of production over hand production are small and where production processes can be atomized and regrouped in labor-intensive chunks (Robinson, 1979: 118-119).

A fourth pull factor can perhaps most charitably be referred to as a "secure business climate" in the semiperipheral countries. It is understandable that businesspersons are sensitive to the risk factor affecting their investments. However, I am not referring primarily to the fear of foreign expropriations here. The "safe" in the phrase "safe business climate" goes well beyond this to include government assurances that social benefits will be kept low, wages "restrained," and favorable tax structures perpetuated. In South Korea, workers do not have the right to strike, and in many other semiperipheral countries political and business leaders are acutely conscious of the linkage between internal reform and foreign capital.

PUSH FACTORS

The sources of peripheral industrialization are not limited to the industrializing countries themselves. Indeed, one prime thesis of this article is that peripheral industrialization is continuously spurred on by changes in the international division of labor and one of the generative sources of this evolving process lies right within the advanced capitalist economies themselves.

The important changes transpiring within advanced capitalist societies concern the transformation of the industrial sector, the changing business environment, the rising costs of labor, and the sharpening of intercapitalist rivalry. The changes occurring within the industrial sectors of advanced capitalist countries are important and include both a shift from industrial production to the provision of services as well as a change in the composition of industrial production itself (Fröbel et al., 1980). This intra-industry shift involves a transition from the labor-intensive, light-manufacturing, and heavy industries to knowledge-intensive, "clean" industries such as microelectronics, computers, and so on. The implication of this shift is that certain traditional manufacturing sectors are, if not becoming obsolete, then at least declining. The decline is expectedly most pronounced in labor-intensive sectors. A study carried out for the U.S. Department of Labor by Michael Aho and Donald Rousslang (1979: Table 2) identifies the twenty industries most negatively affected by trade with LDCs. They include sectors such as textile goods, furniture and fixtures, footwear except rubber, watches, games, and toys, and so on.

A second important push factor concerns the changing environment within which business operates. Aspects of that environment of relevance here are the increasing regulation of business, the existence of stricter controls on pollution (pronounced in the auto industry), health and safety regulations, and the increasing cost of benefits and pensions. While these factors mean increasing costs across the board, they disproportionately affect the labor-intensive industries. Further, there is already evidence, though not of a systematic sort, that many businesspersons feel they are operating in societies where fundamental value changes are taking place, with people placing more emphasis on quality of life than on growth, and seeking to preserve economic and social benefits without regard to market forces.

A third push factor is the rising cost of labor in many advanced countries. During the late 1960s, a series of labor demands led to wage increases in France (after the events of May 1968), in the Netherlands in 1969, and in the United Kingdom after that. In the United States, Canada, and Japan, wages increased rapidly after 1970 (McCracken, 1977: 49-50). Along with rising wages, the indexing of wages to inflation and the "fixed" nature of benefits led many businesspersons to feel that a rigidity characterized the economy and operated in such a way as to prevent productivity from playing a larger role in determining wages.

Part of the push that results in the sending of capital and technology to the semiperiphery originates not within one or several advanced capitalist countries but in the relations among them. This fourth push factor is intercapitalist rivalry. When the United States dominated the capitalist world during the 1950s, market shares were stable and there was little incentive to search for new production sites. Besides, the technological gap between the United States and its closest competitors was large enough to assure large profit margins by maintaining a leading technological position. With a closing of this technological gap and the rise of Germany, Japan, and in some cases Italy and France as major economic competitors of the United States, the significance of third world markets increased. As Warren points out (1973: 14), between 1964 and 1968, U.S. direct and portfolio investment in the Third World as a whole grew by an annual average rate of 15.4%, Japan's at an annual average of 32%, and Germany's at 50%.

Thus, U.S. economic dominance from the end of World War II to the 1960s came to an end and was replaced by a world of several capitalist competitors. Europe, weakened as a result of the war, directed its energies to development and recovery of its internal markets. In doing this, the European Community carried further what the Marshall Plan had started. As it consolidated its hold on internal markets, it directed an increasing portion of its energies to external relations. This meant not only the strengthening of links with former African and Caribbean colonies, but also an attempt to establish links with several Asian and Latin American countries and a flirtation with a Mediterranean policy. Increasingly, the members of the EC came to view the consolidation of their internal markets and international competitiveness as two sides of the same coin.

With the increasing economic presence of various European countries around the globe, the United States and Japan were pressured to step up their paces also, and not out of a sheer "desire to imitate" but out of a necessity not to be undercut in international economic competition. It is this competition, manifesting itself in the export of capital and technology, that has spurred industrialization in the periphery. It is important to recognize that changes within the core did not simply passively allow peripheral industrialization; quite the contrary, this industrialization was positively stimulated by developments in the core, since these developments resulted in external economic policies necessary for the survival of capital in certain sectors.

It is true that some analysts see these "push" factors as short-term phenomena, resting on temporary disturbances within advanced, capitalist economies. The influential "McCracken Report" (McCracken et al., 1977), carried out under the auspices of the Organization for Economic Cooperation and Development (OECD), is the most notable document to set forth this position. The Vietnam War, unattended by appropriate fiscal policies, simultaneous wage "explosions" in Europe and North America, the rising costs of government, the oil price increases, and the monetary expansions of the early 1970s, all contributed to put the brakes on the economy.

In addition to the macroeconomic effects of the above economic disturbances, there are important secular trends occurring within core countries, and these trends are not by and large analyzed by the McCracken Report. Furthermore, there are a number of important longer-term forces at work and these will not be very responsive to the fiscal and monetary policies at the disposal of OECD governments. The Joint Economic Committee of the U.S. Congress (1978), for example, concludes quite differently that "the U.S. is entering a new era in its economic development with circumstances fundamentally different from those of the past." Among the important factors offered in support of this long-term view were the rise of costs of raw materials, the leveling off of gains derived from higher education, the projected slowdown of growth in the labor force, and a "maturing" of some postwar industries (Sewell, 1979: 50). These trends, difficult to manipulate or change in the short run, suggest that the push factors have a more enduring basis than some scholars allow.

FACILITATIVE FACTORS

There are some causes of peripheral industrialization that are not to be found within the semiperiphery or core countries. They "belong," if we must give them a home, to the present state of technology in the global economy. I am speaking of things such as the existence of extensive and integrated communications systems, sophisticated transport facilities, the development of air freight facilities, containerization. These benefits are not free of course; they are controlled by private and public actors. However, they are so much a part of our normal business discourse, so common a support for the international aspects of business, that we can think of them as easing the flow of goods for all, though certainly not with equal benefit.

Four factors have been especially important in facilitating the semiperiphery's ability to utilize the resources potentially available to it: the multinational corporation, technical advances in work organization, subcontracting, and tariff changes.

Huge differences in the supply of capital, technology, and managerial talent have always characterized the center and the periphery. What was needed was an effective and profitable way of delivering packages of capital, technology, and managerial expertise. The multinational corporation, with its mobile capital and technology, worldwide financial networks, sales, and advertising, was particularly appropriate for the job. Although the first and densest wave of multinational corporate activity took place within the advanced capitalist world itself, subsequent surges of transnational investment found outlets among LDCs. This was not only true for the United States, but for other leading capitalist countries as well. West German subsidiaries are located in over seventy countries outside the European Community, but concentrated in Brazil, Spain, the United States, Austria, South Africa, India, Switzerland, Mexico, and Argentina (Fröbel et al., 1978: 137). Japan, anxious since the early 1970s to export the production of resource-intensive, pollution-prone industries abroad, has increasingly located its subsidiaries in neighboring Asian countries such as South Korea, Taiwan, and Thailand (Ozawa, 1979: 159-200).

A second facilitating factor concerns technical "advances"[10] in work organization. Usually mentioned in this category are the fragmentation of the process of production and the development of standard product lines in many different geographical locations. These innovations lend an increasingly modular quality to the work process and its associated technology so that different aspects of production, once integrated within the same work unit and work place, are now "emancipated" to be carried out in different places. This means, in effect, that the rationality (that is, economic rationality) embedded in the ability to take advantage of the most plentiful productive factors can be more intensely exploited. Firms are not so limited as they once were by the

10. I put the word "advances" in quotes since the increasing atomization of the production process would not be considered an advance by many people, especially those not inclined to place economic efficiency at the top of a value hierarchy. However, since my primary interest in this article lies at the intersection of the political and economic sources of economic growth, this process of fragmentation is probably counted as an asset.

necessity of carrying out the entire production of a product in one country; further, they are not constrained to carry out within one workplace different processing phases which might profit from work at several different locations. The differentiation of work and its attendant technology now allow a greater decoupling of work place and labor function and permit the idea of part-processing to proceed at a rapid pace.

The third facilitating factor is the practice of *subcontracting,* which in some ways is the counterpart of part-processing at the levels of law and business practice. The definition of international subcontracting is not clear. Sharpston (1975: 94) defines it broadly to mean "all export sales of articles which are ordered in advance, and where the giver of the order arranges the marketing." Subcontracting can be long-term or short-term, for the purpose of procuring components or limited production processes, and may involve or not involve the transfer of production equipment, capital, and managerial help to the country where the production actually takes place. The common denominator of all these different arrangements is the reliance of the host country firms on the contracting party for sales and marketing.

As I briefly mentioned, international subcontracting must be seen as part of other changes in production within core and peripheral countries. Landsberg (1979: 55), for example, sees the essence of international subcontracting in the cost-cutting advantages of exporting the labor-intensive aspects of production while still controlling such crucial features as product design, technically sophisticated parts of production, and marketing.

The advantages for core countries, that is, for advanced capitalist societies, are substantial. In the semiperiphery, labor productivity is high and wages are low, resulting in low unit costs. In addition, this form of transnational integration of production allows the core to control the pace and direction of technological change, though we should keep in mind that many industries in which subcontracting takes place are technologically stable. Finally, subcontracting occurs only in those parts of the production process wanted by the contracting party and enables the core actors to retain their positions in the high value-added areas.

There are advantages for the semiperiphery too, though these are of a more uncertain nature in the long run. The most important advantage is easy and speedy access to foreign capital and technology, which in combination with local labor creates jobs and generates incomes. Though these incomes are miserable by developed country standards, they are sufficient to attract workers in the local labor markets. Presumably, the gross earnings of these local industries are large enough to allow the local accumulation of capital to take place. In this regard, low wages are put into a very different light.

The semiperipheral actors gain another advantage from international subcontracting. They walk into a ready-made structure of marketing research, advertising, and sales. This is an area in which they would be poorly equipped to compete. Thus, the complementarities between core and semiperipheral countries are strong, and subcontracting provides a mechanism for exploiting these mutually beneficial relationships. However, we should also bear in mind that these benefits may be short-term and they may not encourage rapid or even slow transformation of the economy for the less developed society. Indeed, one can appropriately ask why the core country, benefiting so much from its cheap foreign labor pool and still controlling the highest value-added parts of the production process, would want to relinquish its position. From the standpoint of the semiperiphery, two questions call out for an answer: Must they keep their wages low permanently so as not to lose their special position to the even poorer countries waiting in the wings? And, are they permanently locked into an inferior position in the global division of labor?

The final facilitating factor concerns changes in tariff structures between LDCs and advanced capitalist societies. A long-standing complaint of LDCs has been that tariffs were biased against their industrialization because they increased as the degree of industrial processing increased (Dolan, 1978: 373). Some general improvements have been made with Lomé II providing for more favorable tariffs on industrial exports from LDCs than Lomé I. In addition, the generalized system of preferences, fostered by the United Nations Conference on Trade and Development (UNCTAD), has made some headway.

However, I single out the value-added tariff for attention here. The establishment of this tariff constitutes an important development in international political economy. Again, as with subcontracting, it exploits the cheap labor and ready capital plus markets complementarity between core and semiperiphery. A value-added tariff is a tariff that is levied only on that specific portion of the value of an imported commodity added in the exporting country (Morton and Tulloch, 1977: 184). This, of course, lightens the tariffs on industrial exports from LDCs and encourages the expansion of part-processing activities. It is another mechanism encouraging the increasing modularity of the production process. In this sense, the value-added tariff is the commercial policy equivalent of part-processing activities.

CONVERSION FACTORS

All of the previous factors—push, pull, and facilitative—have the effect of putting considerable resources at the disposal of the semiperipheral countries. How do these resources get converted into output and how is the surplus from this output fed back so that the cycle of production and consumption continues?

In all of these countries, the market plays a strong role. I am not contesting that. What is at least equally striking in almost every case, with the particular exception of Hong Kong and perhaps Singapore, is that the state has played a strong role in shaping the emergence of the semiperiphery (Donges and Riedel, 1975: 61). It has played a strong role in attracting capital, in providing incentives for production in sectors with potential comparative advantage, in channeling scarce funds into industrial sectors, in stimulating exports, and in keeping labor costs low.

Although all of these state actions are important, the stimulation of manufactured exports and simultaneous restructuring of the economy have been the centerpieces of their overall economic strategies. Almost to a country, again with the exception of Hong Kong and to a lesser extent Singapore, the semiperipheral countries went through a period of import-substitution before their outward-looking phase. By the early 1960s, countries such as

Taiwan and South Korea had finished their "easy" phase of substitution and adopted outward-looking policies (Balassa, 1979: 27). Brazil's transition to greater reliance on exports dates from 1966, Mexico's from 1965, Spain's from 1959 (Donges and Riedel, 1975: 61). These dates are not precise, of course, but they do reflect at least the approximate region of this transition.

The stimulation of exports can occur in many ways and domestic policies were not the only instruments in this expansion. The establishment of export processing zones and institution of value-added tariffs are two such examples of externally directed export expansion. However, within the range of instruments that can be affected by the semiperipheral country are exchange rate policy, subsidies to the export sector, tariff exemptions on imports of raw materials and capital goods, preferential interest rates for exporting industries, reduced tax rates on export income, and accelerated depreciation allowances for equipment used for export production.

There are many predicted benign effects associated with export-oriented policies. Improvements in the efficiency of production through specialization in sectors where relative advantages exist, as well as through economies of scale, are two such expectations. Also, the ability to overcome bottlenecks through the easing of balance of payments restrictions on growth plays a role (OECD, 1979: 48). Along these lines, it is important to keep in mind that export-promotion policies require heavy imports of capital goods. It is essential to pay for these imports and still contribute to local accumulation. The opening up of external markets "free[s] key industries from the rigid limitations of the domestic demand pattern" (Keesing, 1979: 13) and allows production to increase partially independently of domestic demand.

Discussion

In this article I have done little more than open up investigation on a complex topic. Many important and difficult questions present themselves. What are the reasons behind the economic growth of the countries studied here? Can this growth be sustained, diversified both horizontally and vertically (that is, into more technologically sophisticated, higher value-added areas), and take place in an equitable fashion? What will be the social consequences of this growth in terms of the weakening of traditionally powerful groups, the ascendance of new elites, and the decline of support groups for political leaders and insitutions? Finally, what implications does rapid economic growth have for political institutions, "regime styles," and leadership? Are liberal institutions at all compatible with rapid peripheral growth or is some form of authoritarianism, from the right or the left, inevitable? These are difficult questions with no easy answers (Duvall and Freeman, 1981).

Some may argue that these questions are not even the "right" ones, that the essay raises too many false problems, and makes too much out of a temporally limited, nonautonomous, and nongeneralizable movement among a few countries. If this is true, the economic growth of the semiperiphery does not deserve the attention bestowed upon it here. There are three limitations of semiperipheral industrialization that are often put forward: limited room for new entrants, limited autonomy of industrialization, and limited ability to change one's position in the global division of labor. These limitations are comprehensive and stringent. Together they fix narrow limits on the movement of less developed societies in their attempt to escape from their present inferior positions.

Perhaps these critics are right in emphasizing the fixed and continuous rather than the variable and discontinuous aspects of the global system. In attributing too much dynamism, too much capacity for self-transformation, to the semiperiphery, one runs the risk of heralding a new era when only an age-old scene is being acted out. However, precisely because these questions are so difficult, and so interlocked, there must be a strategy for investigating them. The danger is that we might jump from a recognition of the importance and interdependence of these questions to a research strategy which attempts to take everything simultaneously into account. While such an approach has some attractions, I do not believe that it offers a realistic route for a comprehensive understanding of peripheral industrialization.

As I see it, there are five major sets of questions that must be posed and much independent theoretical and empirical work needs to be done in each area. Though each question is related to all the others, I propose investigating these questions in the following order. First, what are the reasons for the rise of the semiperiphery, that is, what theory provides a general account of this process? Second, can this process of peripheral development be sustained and expanded, both in sectoral terms within a country and to other countries? Third, can the process of peripheral industrialization become self-transforming, that is, can it become a more autonomous and self-directing form of growth than it presently is? Fourth, what are the implications of peripheral growth for a number of distributional issues, especially those concerning both domestic and international inequality? Fifth, what is the role of the state in the process of economic growth of the periphery? How does the state function to promote (retard) growth, foster (or worsen) equality, and incorporate vs. exclude key elements of society from meaningful participation?

These are important questions, the answers to which are not obvious. Each question implies a considerable amount of theoretical and empirical work. I have tried to open up these investigations with an attempt to shed some theoretical light on the first question. Additional investigations on the issues posed here are no doubt needed before moving to the other, more politically charged issues, on the agenda.

The changes that are occurring on the periphery today may not be revolutionary but they are rapid by historical standards and are resulting in substantial changes. On the southern periphery of Europe, in Spain, Greece, and Portugal, the proportion of the population working in agriculture was cut in half from 1950 to 1970, a reduction which it took the United States six decades to effect (Linz, 1979: 176). Similarly, the rates of growth and economic restructuring on the semiperiphery today are high by historical standards. While we are understandably impatient with poverty and backwardness, it would be counterproductive to underestimate the possibilities for change in the periphery and semiperiphery.

The past twenty years have presented a rich and often conflicting pattern of rapid growth for some with persistent stagnation for others, of authoritarian rule and suppression of elementary human rights in some places (Brazil, South Korea) with moderate political reforms in others (Spain, Portugal), of unchecked economic growth leading to domestic inequalities (Brazil) and strong government intervention to encourage equitable growth in others (South Korea, Taiwan). There are no easy formulas to summarize these wide experiences in each and every case. The general lesson must be supported by individual historical and contextual factors. However, peripheral industrialization provides a fertile laboratory for studying the advantages and opportunities, costs and blind alleys, associated with the rapid economic growth, and, it is hoped, also development, of the less developed world.

Date of receipt of final manuscript: April 28, 1981

REFERENCES

AHO, M. C. and D. J. ROUSSLANG (1979) "The impact of LDC trade on U.S. workers: demographic and occupational characteristics of workers in trade-sensitive industries." U.S. Department of Labor, Office of Foreign Economic Research. Washington, D.C., 1-16.

BALASSA, B. (1979) The Changing International Division of Labor in Manufactured Goods." World Bank Staff Working Paper 329. Washington, DC: World Bank.

BARRATT BROWN, M. (1974) The Economics of Imperialism. Middlesex, England: Penguin Books.

BECKER, J. F. (1977) Marxian Political Economy: An Outline. Cambridge, England: Cambridge Univ. Press.

BREWSTER, H. (1973) "Economic dependence: a quantitative interpretation." Social and Econ. Studies 22, 1: 90-95.

CHENERY, H. B. (1979) "Transitional growth and world industrialization," pp. 457-490 in B. Ohlin et al. (eds.) The International Allocation of Economic Activity. New York: Holmes and Meier.

——— and D. B. KEESING (1979) The Changing Composition of Developing Country Exports. World Bank Staff Working Paper 314. Washington, DC: World Bank.

DOLAN, M. B. (1978) "The Lome' Convention and Europe's relationship with the Third World: a critical analysis." Revue d'Intégration Européenne 1, 3: 369-394.

DONGES, J. B. and J. RIEDEL (1975) "The expansion of manufactured exports in developing countries: an empirical assessment of supply and demand issues." Weltwirtschaftliches Archiv 113, 2: 58-87.

DUVALL, R. D. and J. R. FREEMAN (1981) "The state and dependent capitalism." Int. Studies Q. 25, 1: 99-118.

EVANS, P. (1979) Dependent Development. Princeton, NJ: Princeton Univ. Press.

FRÖBEL, F., J. HEINRICHS, and O. KREYE (1980) The New International Division of Labor. Cambridge, England: Cambridge Univ. Press. (Originally published in the German: (1977) Die Neue Internationale Arbeitsteilung: Strukturelle Arbeitslösigkeit in den Industrieländern und die Industrielisiering der Entwicklungsländer. Hamburg, West Germany: Rowohlt Taschenbach Verlag.)

——— (1978) "The new international division of labor." Social Sci. Information 17, 1: 123-142.

GERSCHENKRON, A. (1962) Economic Development in Historical Perspective. Cambridge, MA: Belknap.

KEESING, D. B. (1979) World Trade and Output of Manufactures: Structural Trends and Developing Countries' Exports. World Bank Staff Working Paper 316. Washington, DC: World Bank.

LANDSBERG, M. (1979) "Export-led industrialization in the Third World: manufacturing imperialism." Rev. of Radical Pol. Economics 11, 4: 50-63.

LINZ, J. (1979) "Europe's southern frontier: evolving trends toward what?" Daedulus 108, 1: 175-209.

McCRACKEN, P. et al. (1977) Towards Full Employment and Price Stability. A report to the OECD by a group of independent experts. Paris: OECD.

MARX, K. (1906) Capital, vol. I. New York: Random House.

MORTON, K. and P. TULLOCH (1977) Trade and Developing Countries. Great Britain: John Wiley.

Organization for Economic Cooperation and Development (1979) The Impact of the Newly Industrializing Countries on Production and Trade in Manufactures. Report by the Secretary General. Paris: Author.

OZAWA, T. (1979) Multinationalism Japanese Style. Princeton, NJ: Princeton Univ. Press.

ROBINSON, J. (1979) Aspects of Development and Underdevelopment. Cambridge, England: Cambridge Univ. Press.

SEWELL, J. S. (1979) "Can the north prosper without growth and development of the south?" pp. 45-76 in M. M. McLaughlin (ed.) The United States and the Third World, Agenda 1979. New York: Praeger.

SHARPSTON, M. (1975) "International subcontracting." Oxford Econ. Papers 27, 1: 94-136.

STOHL, M. and H. TARG (forthcoming) "United States Third World policy: the struggle to make others adapt," in P. Taylor and G. Raymond (eds.) Third World Policies of Industrialized Nations. Boulder, CO: Greenwood Press.

SUNKEL, O. (1973) "Transnational capitalism and national disintegration in Latin America." Social and Econ. Studies 22, 1: 132-176.

United Nations (1976) National Account Statistics. New York: Author.

U.S. Congress, Joint Economic Committee (1978) US Long-Term Economic Growth Prospects: Entering a New Era. Staff Study, 95th Congress, 2nd session, Washington, DC.

U.S. Tariff Commission (1970) Economic Factors Affecting the Use of the Items 807.00 and 806.30 of the Tariff Schedule of the U.S. Washington, DC: Government Printing Office.

WARREN, B. (1973) "Imperialism and capitalist industrialization." New Left Review 81: 3-44.

VERNON, R. (1971) Sovereignty at Bay. New York and London: Basic Books.

——— (1966) "International investment and international trade in the product life cycle." Q. J. of Economics, 80: 190-207.

The Labour Party

Riding the Two Horses

JOHN E. TURNER

Department of Political Science
University of Minnesota

This article deals with the linkages between the parliamentary elite and the activists in the extraparliamentary organization in democratic ideological parties with bifurcated power structures. It shows how cleavages precipitated by changes in the environment of the parliamentary caucus disrupt its penetrative influence over the mass organization, opening up avenues for ideological dissidents who contend for power with the pragmatists in the parliamentary leadership. A framework for the analysis of issue-oriented factional behavior within a defined organizational setting is applied to the British Labour Party in past and contemporary struggles. The author argues that similar studies of elite/activist linkages and ideological splits may be a catalyst for theory development in the political parties field.

Although organizational theorists have tended to neglect it, the Labour Party in Britain is an intriguing type of complex organization which invites closer attention. Two qualities make it an attractive subject to study from an organizational perspective: (1) It is an "ideological" party which is able to win power.[1] (2) It harbors two centers of decision-making—the Party *inside* parliament (the Parliamentary Labour Party, or PLP) and the mass organization *outside* of parliament. Since the Labour partisans have been unable to agree on which of the two cores of authority carries the greater weight, the organization has never established

---

1. Scholars disagree on the definition of an ideological political movement/party. The author categorizes the Labour Party as an ideological organization because it claims allegiance to a set of values and beliefs that presents a diagnosis of the ills of the existing

---

AUTHOR'S NOTE: The author gratefully acknowledges the comments and suggestions offered to him by his colleagues: Professors Robert T. Holt, Robert Kvavik, and W. Phillips Shively, and by two stimulating advisees, Professor Bruce Williams and Ms. Vicki Templin.

INTERNATIONAL STUDIES QUARTERLY, Vol. 25 No. 3, September 1981 385-437
© 1981 I.S.A.

a *formal mechanism* with commanding power to resolve the policy differences between them.

These two qualities in combination tend to breed conflict: ideological disagreements are obviously harder to contain in an organizational structure that does not specify clearly where sovereignty lies. Dissidents who lose the battle in one power center are in a position to carry the struggle to the other political arena. This is the situation that has long existed in the Labour Party. Tensions have often emerged between the leaders of the parliamentary group, who are inclined toward a pragmatic approach, and a more ideological minority which forges linkages with "leftist-leaning" elements in the Party's external units. During an early episode of left/right contention, James Maxton, a "stormy petrel" from the Clydeside, made an off-the-cuff comment which portrayed the difficulty of managing a fissiparous organization: "if the leader can't ride two horses at once, then he should not be in the bloody circus" (in Hatfield, 1973).

The purpose of this article is to examine the impact of policy differences upon a political organization with divided authority patterns. In this inquiry, we shall address several questions: How does a political organization ordinarily resolve the problem of decision-making when the policy-making authority is ambiguously distributed between the parliamentary group and the external units? What factors arise to disturb this normal pattern, thus assisting the cause of the dissident elements in the organization? In what ways does the disturbance of the balanced pattern affect

social order and offers a program of action, embedded in the belief system, which aims at a basic reconstruction of socioeconomic relationships in the entire society (see Turner, 1978: 5, 330 footnote 3). Throughout this essay, the author refers to the "left-wing" of the party, which is hard to define precisely because the differences between "left" and "right" are to some extent a matter of degree. The leftists usually have more intense, emotional feelings about the class-based elements of the belief system, and, impatient with gradualism, demand more extreme changes to be instituted at a more rapid pace. The *leftist syndrome* in the Labour Party consists of the following programmatic features: more radical intervention by the state in economic affairs through various forms of public ownership and control; a "massive and irreversible shift" in the distribution of wealth; import controls; worker participation in industrial management; rejection of an incomes policy; Britain's withdrawal from the Common Market; unilateral nuclear disarmament; Britain's withdrawal from the NATO alliance; immediate abolition of the House of Lords; the use of industrial action as a supplement to parliamentary action; and so forth. Perhaps the most salient characteristic is this: most of the people who are described as "leftists" in this essay would proudly locate themselves in the left-wing camp.

the behavior of the actors in the two wings of the organization? After erecting a rudimentary framework to guide the analysis, we shall turn our attention to the British Labour Party. Our objective is to examine the ways in which it has characteristically handled the problem of bifurcated authority, to discern the factors that are disrupting the equilibrium in its structure, and to assess the impact of these disturbances upon the norms that have traditionally governed the behavior of its members in the House of Commons. To synopsize the situation in Maxton's metaphoric language, straddling the two horses has become a difficult feat for the Party Leader because in recent years one of the horses—the extraparliamentary organization—has been trotting out of control.

Framework of Analysis

The application of this study is restricted to ideological parties in democratic countries, and the framework is designed primarily for the analysis of political organizations in two-party systems.[2] A multiparty environment affects the operation of parties in distinctive ways, largely because of the need to form coalition governments and because the list method of candidate selection is ordinarily employed. But even in multiparty systems with these discriminating features, the study has some applicability.

Parties with a strong external structure originated outside of parliament, long after suffrage was expanded; their task was to develop a mass organization which would enable them to establish a foothold in the legislative chambers. Needless to say,

2. The genesis of the framework is partly inductive and partly deductive. Over the years, the author has written about political organizations in Britain, the United States, Japan, and the USSR, and as a coauthor of a more recent work on American politics in comparative perspective, he cursorily examined the operation of selected political parties in Western Europe, Scandinavia, and some Commonwealth countries. A few months ago, he spent considerable time at his desk addressing such questions as: What keeps the component units of ideological parties together? How do they become "unhooked"? What happens when the competing forces within these organizations begin to work at cross-purposes? Obviously, the reading program covering a wide range of cases represents an "inductive experience" which was filtered into the psyche and had an impact on the resulting framework which displays rough deductive features.

most of these parties are of left-wing persuasion, functioning on a working-class base. Political organizations of the right, even when they were created outside of the legislature, are not so troubled with the problem of bifurcated authority.[3]

Conflict is enduring in all political parties that emphasize ideological creeds. It is probably less consequential in right-wing organizations, however, because reverence for order and deference to authority are embedded in the ideology. Parties of the left, on the other hand, are not inhibited by such constraints, and disaccord over precepts and programs appears to be more characteristic of their internal affairs. For this reason, left-wing organizations with an ideological focus will capture the central spotlight in this study.

Since an ideological party tends to draw its activists from the most ambitious, the most aggressive, and the most doctrinaire elements of the population, it is hardly surprising that such an organization becomes an arena for personal and ideological skirmishes. Cleavages develop between the "ideologists" and the "pragmatists," between those who cling to the basic principles of the creed and favor speedy advance toward the party's goals, and those who are willing to trim the doctrine and to proceed at a slower, more cautious pace. This ideological split evolves in both the parliamentary group and the mass organization. Within the legislative caucus, the doctrinal enthusiasts inevitably clash with a leadership inclined toward a pragmatic course as it develops its strategies to deal with day-to-day problems. The dissidents often receive a warmer reception in the nonlegislative branch of the party, which attracts many activists whose political views are more extreme than those of the voters who support the party at the polls.

A political party is not a "closed system" but is embedded in an environment which often changes rapidly and to which it must adapt if it is to perform successfully (Thompson, 1967). The environment of the parliamentary group is made up of two components: (1) the party's mass organization; and (2) the range

3. See Duverger, 1954: xxx-xxxii, 170-171, 238. In the following pages of this section, the author has been influenced by the Duverger analysis.

of groups with which it must deal, depending upon whether it is in opposition or whether it is called upon to form a government. The linkage between the two components merits brief discussion.

The parliamentary leaders must always deal with the mass organization. It is viewed as the democratic base of the party, the nesting ground of the activists who take on the tedious, unexciting tasks and whose views must at least be listened to, if not always heeded. The external party is the connecting link between the parliamentary group and the voters, and it cannot safely be ignored.

When the party sheds its opposition role and moves into the government offices, the parliamentary leaders have more resources at their command and are less dependent upon the outside organization. They not only have posts to distribute, but they also can appeal to party loyalty on the ground that rebellion in the ranks weakens the government and plays into the hands of the political enemy.

The breadth of the new responsibilities of the party leaders encourages them to make a more compelling claim for decision-making autonomy. As de facto rulers of the realm, they have to be concerned with the welfare of the entire nation, not just with the views of the activists in the external wing of their movement. They are now called upon to deal directly with a wide array of groups and interests which they have hitherto been able to disregard: the civil service and other parts of the executive, pressure groups which are not in tune with their own philosophy, foreign governments with different political outlooks, and so on. They soon discover that the political world extends over a broader domain; it is not as simple as the one portrayed in the tracts they published when they were in opposition. Carrying the seals of governmental office, the party chieftains quickly discern that some of the policies incubated in the traditional doctrine are basically unworkable. Wider decision latitude affords them opportunities to pick and choose among alternatives so as to avoid alienating particular clienteles whose electoral support will help them to win another term. All of these considerations induce the parliamentary leaders to move cautiously, charting their course by the buoys of pragmatism rather than by the beacon lights of doctrine. These deviations from prescribed routes naturally arouse the hostility of the ideologists who see themselves as the guardians of the true faith.

The parliamentary group loses some of its advantaged position when it relinquishes office and moves into opposition. Having lost the political resources it commanded when it was at the helm, it is now more dependent upon the external party in its effort to recoup the electoral losses. Moreover, the parliamentary leaders no longer enjoy the glamor and prestige of office; indeed, they are vulnerable to the charge that their policies lost the support of the local activists as well as the voters.

Having discussed the environment of the party's parliamentary group, we are ready to view the main guideposts of the study. The roughhewn framework is made up of three parts: (1) a description of how a political organization with a forked power structure resolves the problem of decision-making when it is in a stable condition; (2) an examination of the factors that disturb the regular pattern; and (3) an analysis of the impact of the changing distribution of power upon the organization.

RESOLUTION OF THE DECISION-MAKING PROBLEM UNDER STABLE CONDITIONS

The parliamentary cluster and the extraparliamentary component are heavily dependent upon each other. The parliamentary group views the external party as the pipeline to the electorate and relies upon it for manpower resources and financial support, while the mass organization depends upon the parliamentary wing for the articulation of finely tuned policy and its enactment into law. In some political systems, the parties are decentralized, with weak external organizations, and the members of the parliamentary unit are virtually unrestrained in carrying out their legislative functions. If coherent policy-making takes place at all, it is done in the parliamentary caucus, perhaps in collaboration with the chief executive. The external party usually presents its greatest threat to the parliamentarians at election time by challenging their renomination.

The situation is more complicated when the mass organization is well developed, because the two wings are in a position to compete with each other for power. Since the organization's effectiveness will be jeopardized when it attempts to speak with two voices, some arrangement has to be worked out so that the decision-making authority is clearly delineated. This can be done in one of two ways: (1) a mechanism is created for negotiating the differences between the two interdependent components, or (2) the organization establishes a hierarchy in which one unit is clearly subordinated to the authority of the other. If the external party becomes the dominant element, the members of the parliamentary group are transformed into *mandated delegates* who are constrained in their capacity to adapt to changing or unforeseen circumstances in the legislative arena. If the parliamentary wing is given a commanding role, the external party suffers a decline in prestige and tends to become a vestigial policy-making structure.

Even when a political party has a strong mass organization, there is a distinct tendency for the parliamentary group to become the dominant unit. Since the governing organs of the external party meet infrequently and for only short periods of time, they lack the capacity to monitor the daily activities and decisions of the legislative caucus. Besides, the delegates to these assemblies have insufficient information about the problems that have to be tackled and command little knowledge of the contextual interlacing of these problems. Nor are they in a position to anticipate all of the problems that require on-the-spot decisions. Furthermore, in some political systems, constitutional norms prohibit an outside organization from issuing voting instructions to its legislative representatives on the assumption that they are to be independent members of a deliberative assembly. Even when the authoritative body of the external wing delegates its monitoring responsibility to a subsidiary organ which meets more frequently, the basic difficulties still remain.

The party's representatives in the legislative cluster are not so handicapped when they are called upon to deal with important issues. They are in a much better position to gather and process information, and their closer view of a wider picture enables them to perceive available options and to forecast the consequences of alternative policies. Interacting with each other over extended periods of time, the legislators are positioned to deal with the unforeseen, to share information, and to engage in a thorough discussion of issues. Since they function in the official decision-making arena, the public spotlight is on them, and their roles attract attention and prestige.

The glare of publicity is focused particularly upon the leader of the parliamentary group who is clearly a national figure eligible to be chosen as the head of the executive branch. This responsibility for the entire party stimulates a desire for leeway in the formulation of policies which will be attractive to the electorate and in the designing of parliamentary strategies which will be a challenge to the opposition. This means that the leader and lieutenants will resist any constraints that the mass organization seeks to impose upon them.

Even though in full command of the legislative caucus, the leader cannot afford to have the parliamentary group get noticeably out of step with the external party. This is not a problem when the anatomy of the mass organization is so weak that it cannot effectively monitor the behavior of its legislators, or when the party's rules clearly lodge the decision-making authority in the parliamentary contingent. The problem can become serious, however, in the case of a political organization that has a competitive external wing and is forced to operate under either of two structural conditions: (1) a mechanism for negotiating concerted action exists and has to be employed; or (2) the jurisdictional boundaries are not definitely marked out and there is no mechanism for adjusting divergent claims. We are mainly concerned with those ideological parties in which the domains of authority between the parliamentary wing and the external units are ill-defined and there is an absence of machinery for resolving conflicts.

A party with these properties is forced to operate within a complex environment. The parliamentary leaders are called upon to deal with a mass organization whose basic outlook may be incongruent not only with the approach of a majority of the caucus, but also with the attitudes of the party's voters. In order to prevent the external cluster from working at cross purposes with the parliamentary group, the legislative leaders will attempt to develop informal political influence in the organs of the external party.

INSTABILITY IN THE DECISION-MAKING STRUCTURE

Several factors may intervene to disturb the equilibrium in a political party whose blurred lines of decision-making authority require mediation between the two power centers or penetration of the mass organization by the parliamentary group. These factors fall into two categories, environmental and programmatic, and the two are usually interrelated.

Environmental Factors. Two types of environmental change may emerge to upset the decision-making balance in an ideological party with divided authority patterns. The first type is change in the structure of the external party's authoritative organs so that its "mood"—and often its stand on issues—is modified. This change may be precipitated by: (1) shifts in the leadership of the component units, with the result that the new wielders of power advance different policies for their organizations; and (2) alterations in the relative power position of the constituent elements, as, for example, when a trade union declines in strength or when several unions amalgamate. If the change in the external party affects the parliamentary group adversely, the mechanism for hammering out compromises between the two structures will work less smoothly; or, in cases where no formal mechanism exists, the informal controls exercised by the parliamentary leaders over the external units are rendered ineffectual.

The second type of environmental change involves the transformation of the organization from an opposition party into a party of government and back again. When the party moves into public office, its leaders become more insulated from the pressure of the external units and tend to assume an autonomous posture. In their new roles as guardians of the national welfare, they sometimes must introduce policies that are unpopular with the activists in the mass organization. When this happens, serious challenges are issued in the nonparliamentary arena.

When the party moves back into opposition and returns to the ordinary routines of operation, the leaders lose most of their independent political resources and relinquish some of their claims to autonomy which may have been justified by the responsibilities of office. Now in closer touch with the party activists and more dependent upon them, they are willing to make more concessions to the mass organization.

Programmatic Factors. In an ideological party with competing power centers, the strategic variable in the disruption of its steady state is divisive issues. For reasons already given, the ideologists are ordinarily in the minority in the parliamentary group; the pragmatic course pursued by the leaders commands the support of a majority of the legislators, at least in part because their careers are tied to the existing configuration of power. The inferior position of the ideologists in the caucus prompts them to search for allies in the governing organs of the external party. Under ordinary circumstances, however, the seeds they plant do not yield a bountiful harvest. Many working-class delegates are more interested in "bread and butter" issues than in the fine threads of doctrine; in any event, the penetration of the external party by the leadership tends to neutralize the efforts of the opposition.

The issues that disturb the equilibrium in the party fall into two categories. The first type includes issues of strong emotive or doctrinal appeal which sweep through the movement, attracting people who are ordinarily found in the moderate camp. We can cite as examples the church-state question, a proposal to ban nuclear weapons or to reduce armaments, or a plan to bring more industries into public ownership. Such issues, which may appear and disappear suddenly, play into the hands of the ideologists who temporarily benefit from increased voting strength both in the parliamentary group and in the organs of the external party and are thus in a better position to harass the leadership. An issue of emotional intensity may have an impact upon the structure of the authoritative organs of the external party, especially when it agitates the movement to the extent of affecting delegate selection to the representative bodies, thereby weakening the leaders' control over them.

The second type of issue is the "bread and butter" variety. When the party leaders adopt policies that are perceived to be inimical to the interests of particular clienteles, especially during periods of financial stress, the moderates in both the parliamentary and the external wings of the party immediately grow concerned. People who display no dogmatic attachment to doctrine become very sensitive to measures that shrink their pocketbooks. In the event of such a crisis, the pragmatists are thrown into uneasy coalition with the ideological enthusiasts, and the changing distribution of power within the structure poses a serious threat to the party's high command. This type of situation usually arises when the party is in power. If the adverse policies continue to be advanced over a period of years, they (like a salient emotive issue) are likely to feed back into the structure of the governing organs of the external party through delegate selection to its representative bodies, rendering them less amenable to penetration and negotiation.

IMPACT OF THE CHANGING DISTRIBUTION OF POWER

If the dissidents gain significant control over the mass organization, they will attempt to transfer their power to the parliamentary area. This involves two strategies: (1) influencing the selection of parliamentary candidates so that those chosen will be sympathetic with the dissidents' position, and (2) controlling the renomination of incumbents so that they will be more accountable to the components of the external party and less accountable to the leaders of the parliamentary group.

A successful effort on the part of the rebels may be unbearable for many of the pragmatists, and they may decide to withdraw from the organization. Since they are located closer to the center of the political spectrum, they at least stand a chance of remaining politically effective either by establishing a new party that will

PARLIAMENTARY GROUP

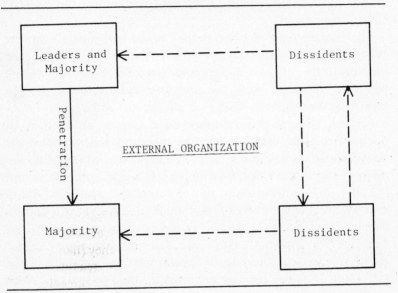

Figure 1: Party in Steady State

have an appeal to mainstream voters, or by joining the other major party. These are options that are not open to left-wing dissidents who want to continue to make a political impact: they cannot, on ideological grounds, move into the other major party, and entry into an organization farther to the left would leave them with only splinter support at the polls.

SUMMARY

In this crude framework for the study of ideological parties with two power centers, the dependent variable is the power of the external organization, as displayed in the strength of its structures and its ability and willingness to defy the party leadership. Under ordinary circumstances, the independent variable is the penetration of the outside units by the parliamentary leaders through informal political influence (see Figure 1).

However, the degree of penetration (which influences the power of the mass organization) is affected by changes in the party's *environment:*

(1) Change in the *structure* of the authoritative organs of the external party occasioned by ordinary shifts in the leadership of the constituent units and by alterations in the relative power position of the constituent units, both of which promote modifications in policy stands.

(2) Change in the role of the party.

(a) When the party is the government, its leaders have great political resources at their command in terms of posts to be filled and policies to be enacted and implemented, and as custodians of the entire nation they can lay claim to autonomy. Moreover, they can appeal to party loyalty because the local activists incur losses if their government is weakened by unrelenting criticism. On the other hand, the leaders have less time to nurture the mass organization, and the imperatives of governing often result in unpopular policies.

(b) When the party is in opposition, the leaders suffer a depletion of political resources, their claim to autonomy are less viable, and they grow more dependent upon the local partisans in the external units.

The degree of penetration (which influences the power of the mass organization) is also affected by *programmatic* factors. The emergence of controversial issues may be so compelling within the external organization that the parliamentary leaders are no longer able to control it through the penetrative and negotiation process. Issues of strong emotive and doctrinal appeal or "bread and butter" questions (which are more apt to arise when the party is in power) may capture the enthusiasm of the activists, prompting some of the moderates to link arms with the ideologists so that they can exert pressure on the party's high command. If the issues have strong enough allurement and are sustained over time, opposing stands become the basis for selecting delegates to the governing bodies of the external organization, thereby feeding back into its structure and precipitating change in the extraparliamentary units (see Figure 2).

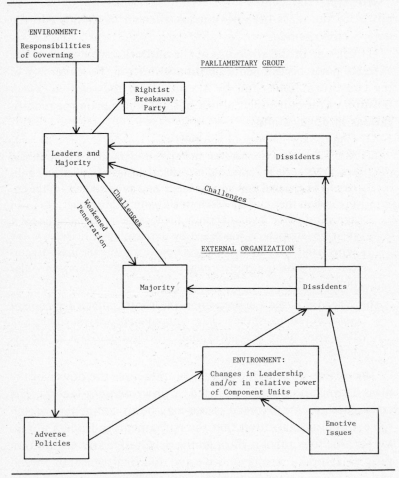

Figure 2: Party in Disequilibrium

The Labour Party in its "Steady State"

The configuration of a political party is frequently specified by the circumstances of history. In contrast to the Conservatives and the Liberals, the Labour Party was established by political forces outside of parliament, and it took the form of a loose federation of trade unions and socialist societies, along the lines of the Trades Union Congress. In 1918, a set of constituency organizations enrolling individual members was attached to the federation to create the four-dimensional alliance which exists today: the trade unions, one cooperative organization, the socialist societies, and the constituency parties.

The governing body of the Labour Party outside of parliament is the Annual Conference: an assembly of approximately 1170 delegates who represent the constituency parties and the affiliated organizations in proportion to the size of their memberships. Since the Conference employs the unit rule ("block vote"), with the voting strength of each organization being determined by the number of members who are affiliated with the Party, the trade unions wield tremendous influence. At the 1979 conference, for example, they commanded 90% of the votes.[4] But even without the block vote, the unions would have notable balloting strength. The trade union power is concentrated in the five or six largest unions whose combined voting allotment (if their leaders stick together) can result in majority control.

Since the Party Conference meets only once a year (and for only a few days), it relies heavily upon the National Executive Committee (NEC) to carry out its decisions. The 29 members, who ordinarily meet together once each month, are largely drawn from the several elements of the federation. The trade unions occupy twelve of the seats, and their representatives are nominated by the unions and voted upon by the union delegates to the Conference. In similar fashion, the delegates from the constituency parties elect the seven NEC members to which they are entitled. One seat is filled by the delegates from the cooperatives and the socialist societies, and one seat is reserved for the Young Socialists who select their representative at their own conference. The Party Leader and his deputy serve as ex-officio members. The six remaining members (the Party Treasurer and five women representatives) may be nominated by any of the affiliated organizations, but they are voted upon by the entire Conference. This means that the people who secure these positions are those who can win the support of the unions. Thus, with their own

4. See Report of the Seventy-Eighth Annual Conference of the Labour Party (1979: 164). (Hereafter, this source will be cited as Annual Conference Report.)

twelve seats and Conference-wide voting power over six others, the trade unions can, if enough of them act in concert, lay claim to 18 of the 29 memberships on the NEC. This body can be influential because it not only looks after the organizational health of the Party, but it also conducts studies of salient issues, formulates policy statements, and structures the agenda for the Conference debates.

Competing with the external organization is the Parliamentary Labour Party, which includes all of the Labour MPs. Meeting once a week or every fortnight, it makes binding decisions on the policies that the Labour members are to support, as well as on the strategies to be followed in parliamentary maneuvers. As is well known, each Labour MP is expected to honor the PLP decisions and to march into the appropriate division lobby when the votes are taken. Although a person is entitled to *abstain* on matters of "deeply held personal conscientious conviction," a vote *against* the Party's decision is usually regarded as a political sin, and the rules give the PLP the authority to withdraw the whip from "rebels" who persist in violating discipline.

That portion of the PLP's environment which consists of the external party is heterogeneous and complex. The Labour leaders have to contend with a Party Conference which represents the various elements of the federation and presumably speaks for the activists at the grassroots. The authority of the Conference is deeply rooted in the culture of the Labour movement and commands great respect among the rank-and-file members. For many of them, the Conference is the "parliament of the movement" which has the final say in policy matters and can claim the right to issue directives to the Labour MPs. Viewing the party inside parliament as merely the creature of the mass organization, they reject its declaration of autonomous status, and they deeply resent having their leaders adopt policies and enforce policy stands that contradict the expressed will of the Conference, even when the Party is in power. Traditionally, the Labour Party has managed to gather support largely by being critical, and it is difficult for the activists to discard their opposition outlook when their organization wins office. At the Conference, the activists openly express their opinions, and with salient issues under review a Labour government is bound to come under some attack. Between Conference sessions, of course, the Party leadership has to deal with the National Executive Committee.

Thus, the Labour Party shelters two important cores of authority, the parliamentary caucus and the external organization, and the relationship between them has never been definitively clarified. The Party Constitution is ambiguous as to which group speaks with an authentic voice when their policies clash, and no effective mechanism has been established for the reconciliation of their differences. The Party Leader has always faced the problem of keeping the two horses in step.

The Two Horses in Step

The early history of the Labour Party was marked by considerable tension between its parliamentary and extraparliamentary wings, but after it began to recover from its defeat in 1931 and had taken a clear position on the collective security issue at the 1935 Conference, the two components of the organization entered a period of relatively smooth relationships which lasted until the end of the Attlee Government in 1951.[5] The working arrangement was based upon an uneasy compromise which had emerged at the 1907 Conference and which has served as a refuge for later parliamentary leaders: resolutions passed by the governing body of the mass organization were to be regarded as the opinions of the Conference, but the timing and method of carrying them out were to be left to the Parliamentary Party. In other words, the norm was established that the Conference is entitled to draw broad outlines of policy for the Party as a whole, but the PLP has the right to interpret the policies and to determine the priorities and the timing of the legislation it introduces.[6]

5. The best analysis of the Labour Party from an historical perspective is presented in McKenzie (1963). See especially Chapter 7.

6. See, for example, the statement of Aneurin Bevan (Annual Conference Report, 1958: 214); the statement of A. Len Williams (Annual Conference Report, 1960: 165-167); Morgan Phillips (1960: 3-4); the issues of New Statesman from June 30, 1961 through July

The period of calm is best explained by the efforts of the parliamentary leaders, in the absence of a formal mechanism for fostering cohesion between the two wings, to penetrate the external party by informal political influence. This penetration was achieved in two ways. The PLP leaders commanded the support of the larger trade union delegations which cast the lion's share of the votes at the Party Conference. Effective influence upon the strong delegations helped to insure Conference approval of official policies when they were put to a vote. The parliamentary chieftains also benefited from the election of important Labour MPs to the National Executive Committee, a strategem that placed it under the sway of people who were committed to the supremacy of the parliamentary group.[7]

The penetration technique was clearly evident during the Attlee regime. In the elections for the 27 seats on the National Executive Committee between 1946 and 1950, the number of MPs who were declared the winners ranged from sixteen to seventeen; within this group, the number of ministers varied from seven to eleven.[8] In several respects, the year 1946 was the most threatening to the parliamentary leadership during the Attlee period; yet its predominance was clearly evident at the Party Conference. The delegates voted against the recommendations of the MP-dominated National Executive Committee on four occasions, but none of the defeats involved a significant issue. The sharpest daggers were thrown at Ernest Bevin, the Foreign Secretary, who faced five hostile resolutions during the debate on foreign policy. But he was in full command of the situation: two of them were withdrawn, and the other three were voted down (Annual Conference Report 1946: 150-169; and Table 1, this essay). During this period, the informal political influence exerted by the parliamen-

---

28, 1961; and the more recent statement by James Callaghan (Annual Conference Report, 1979: 228-229). In the 1945 election campaign, Winston Churchill charged that the Labour Party's external organization could issue instructions to the PLP; Attlee's reply was printed in *The Times* (July 3, 1945).

7. The rapport between the parliamentary leaders and the spokesmen of the big unions had been a characteristic of the Labour Party during the interwar years, and MPs had long been a dominating influence on the NEC (see McKenzie, 1963: 421-426).

8. These figures have been tabulated from the NEC lists given in the annual Conference reports. The MPs serving on this body were checked against the author's data files, which cover the period 1945-1980.

tary leadership upon the mass organization was effective, and, compared with what happened later, the two horses were easy to ride.

The Two Horses Drift Apart

During the Attlee years, rumblings of discontent could be heard both in the Parliamentary Labour Party and at the Conference, but they never grew loud enough to be threatening. The socialist government had managed to place on the statute books virtually all of the domestic reforms the Party had advocated since 1918; this fact tended to compensate for the policies that drew criticism. But such a counterbalance was no longer possible after 1951. With the main planks in its platform nailed down, the organization faced the questions: What do we do next? Where do we go from here? The Labour Party had never constructed a coherent theoretical framework; the diverse groups under its canopy were inclined to define socialism in terms of particular doctrinal tenets to which they had an emotional or intellectual attachment. An ideological party is vulnerable to schism, but when the doctrine is loosely drawn, the pragmatists enjoy wider latitude and the potential for schism is greater.

In the absence of a clear blueprint for the next stage of development, the situation was ripe for the operation of programmatic factors. Desirous of having the Labour Party returned to office as soon as possible, some of its intellectual leaders sought to recast the doctrine in a mold more relevant to the contemporary British scene.[9] Labour, in their view, was now called upon to come to terms with problems that the traditional creed had not envisaged and consequently offered no guidelines. The Attlee reforms, they believed, had changed the face of British society. For this reason, they were convinced that the Party had to discard its depression mentality and develop a program that would be

9. See, for example, Crosland (1960; 1953). For Hugh Gaitskell's diagnosis of the problem, see Annual Conference Report (1959: 105-114). Minkin (1978) presents an excellent analysis of the impact of revisionism (see especially Chapter 10). Minkin's work is a first class study of Labour Party politics.

more attractive not only to workers who now enjoyed a comfortable lifestyle, but also to voters who located themselves in the middle class. These revisionist notions kindled resentment in some sections of the PLP and among many partisans in the mass organization. For these dissenters, revisionism hatched in the nest of pragmatism was the equivalent of heresy, infecting the roots and branches of pure socialism.

The ideological confusion made the Party vulnerable to shifting moods, and for more than a decade after 1952 the doctrinaire elements in both the parliamentary caucus and the external party increased their strength as a result of several emotive issues which convulsed the organization. The first of these was the "Bevanite" movement, a left-wing thrust directed by a minority group of Labour MPs. By 1952, the dissidents had managed to win six of the seven seats in the constituency party section of the National Executive Committee, replacing party leaders of long standing. This marked a change in the environment of the Parliamentary Labour Party: The structure of the external organization was modified, and the leadership since that time has not been able to rely on the guaranteed support of an important group of MPs on the NEC. The Bevanites, however, were never able to penetrate deeply into the trade unions; hence, the PLP leaders could still command backing from the big labor organizations when their policies were being voted on at the Conference and at NEC meetings.

The second wave of unrest was stimulated by the issue of public ownership of industry, a commitment that has long been inscribed on the Party's spiritual tablets. Stung by the election defeat in 1959, Hugh Gaitskell, the Party Leader, suggested that Labour should shake off its "cloth cap" image by loosening its dogmatic attachment to nationalization. This stirred the wrath of the doctrinal enthusiasts, and when many trade unionists, ordinarily loyal to the leadership, joined the protesters, Gaitskell was forced to lay his proposal aside.

While the rebellion over public ownership was still simmering, the partisans of the left were able to seize upon a new emotional issue which had surfaced in the arena of struggle: unilateral nuclear disarmament. In the meantime, another structural change had taken place in the external party. Some of the larger trade unions, through the normal turnover of leadership, had installed new officials at the head of their organizations. These chieftains exerted as much influence as their predecessors but often viewed political issues from a different perspective. This changeover in union leadership resulted in a major shift in the balance of forces within the external units, and the loss of dependable support greatly weakened the penetrative influence of the high command in the Parliamentary Party. Its diminished power in the mass organization was especially noticeable at the 1960 Conference which, as a result of the transfer of some trade union support to the dissenting camp, voted to commit the Party to a policy of unilateralism, handing the parliamentary leaders their first defeat on a *major* issue in the postwar period. (Annual Conference Report, 1960: 170-202).

The shift of the Party away from its stable state dramatizes the problem of competing power centers advocating discordant policies. The Conference decision placed the majority of the Labour MPs in an awkward position. They had been elected on a contrary platform, and the Parliamentary Party had taken an official stand against unilateralism just a few months earlier. Were they now to reverse field in conformity with the Conference mandate, or should they defy its action (Annual Conference Report, 1960: 162-163)? On the other hand, the unilateralist MPs, who constituted about 20% of the parliamentary group, now had the authority of the Conference behind them and could justify their violations of discipline on defense questions.

Although Gaitskell asserted the autonomy of the Parliamentary Party, he launched a vigorous campaign to get the decision reversed. By the time the 1961 Conference was called to order, he had managed to persuade some of the trade union leaders to change their position on the unilateralist issue, and the vote was turned the other way. The Party Leader was sensitive to the need to have the Conference and the PLP in congruence, and by stirring the Conference to change its enunciated policy, he was implicitly recognizing the authentic voice of the mass organization.

As the Labour Party advanced into the 1960s, then, the grip of its leaders on NEC seats held by loyalist MPs had been loosened and some of the big trade unions were wavering in their allegiance. So long as a party occupies an opposition role, the leadership can afford to give way to the feelings of the activists on some issues, and it can seek to avoid head-on clashes by having decisions postponed or by taking refuge in the ambiguous wording of policy statements. But these options are largely foreclosed when the party wins office. Then its leaders have to face up to problems and put forward concrete proposals, and they are accountable, not just to the mass organization, but to the entire country.

Outer Horse Tugs at The Harness

After the 1961 Conference, which gave the Party leaders the policy reversal they wanted on unilateralism but defeated them twice on other defense issues, the governing body of the external organization remained quiescent. The reasons for this are obvious: Harold Wilson replaced Gaitskell as Leader in 1963, the Party began to prepare for the 1964 election, and Labour's razor-thin majority in that election alerted the stalwarts to the realization that another electoral struggle was not far away.

When Wilson became Prime Minister in 1964 (with a slender majority) and in 1966 (with a very comfortable margin), he and his colleagues were caught between the responsibilities of governing a troubled nation and the demands of the militants in the mass organization. These cross-pressures were much more threatening than those that had confronted the first postwar Labour Government. The Attlee regime had had to compromise the ideology as it set about to direct the reconstruction of the economy, but the sacrifices demanded were counterbalanced by economic and social reforms which were in tune with traditional doctrine.

Wilson and his successor, James Callaghan, faced a much different set of problems, however, and there was little agreement within the Party on which ideological signposts should guide their course. The economy was marred by spiraling inflation, swelling unemployment, and lagging growth rates. Within the Party, pressures mounted for the continued expansion of social benefits, but Britain's capacity to provide them had seriously diminished. By the mid-1960s, the Party leaders had come to realize that improvements in the social services and wage packets expanding in excess of increases in worker productivity had to give way to policies designed to strengthen the economy.

PROGRAMMATIC FACTORS

Once again programmatic factors were moved to the front of the Labour stage. Emotional issues involving defense policy, foreign policy, and public ownership kept emerging intermittently and were argued out in both the PLP and the Party Conference. But what brought a surge of resistance to the Party leaders was their austerity program, which affected the purses of ordinary citizens. The ideological enthusiasts were especially vocal in their criticism of the Government's actions, and the unpopular measures gave them the ammunition they needed in their search for allies. The rebels' appeals to protect the social services won increased support for them among the moderates in the parliamentary group, and their successes were even more pronounced when they carried the battle to the mass organization.

The broadening schism between the parliamentary leaders and the Labour backbenchers in the House of Commons can be portrayed by the increased violations of Party discipline. As mentioned earlier, the defiance of a three-line whip (even by abstaining) except for reasons of conscience is viewed as a serious matter. From the beginning of the Attlee regime through the resignation of Callaghan, the number of instances in which at least 5% of the backbench MPs defied three-line whips is as follows:[10]

	IN GOVERNMENT	IN OPPOSITION
1945-1965	15	9
(20½ years)		
1966-1979	51	4
(13 1/3 years)		

The discord between the leadership of the parliamentary group and the mass organization can be gauged in rough measure by the number of hostile resolutions on important policies that were passed by the Conference against the wishes of the Party chieftains. For the Conference delegates to go on record in opposition to a major policy of the leaders—and especially a Labour Government—is an unusual and serious event. As we have observed, the few rebellions during the Attlee years involved minor issues. The first upsets of the leadership on major issues in the postwar period occurred in 1960-1961 when the Party was in opposition; all six of these centered on the defense question which was evoking an emotional reaction in the movement at the time. What must be recognized as a new and significant development in the history of the Labour Party is this: Since 1966, the Conference has become a persistent challenger of its leaders, delivering two or three defeats to them at each Conference and sometimes six or seven, even when they were in charge of the government with either a tiny majority or no majority at all[11] (see Table 1). Note that after 1966, the critical motions were increasingly on "material" as against "ideological" issues. This fact indicates that the left has made considerable gains among the working-class elements within the Party. The PLP's penetration of the external organization has reached the weakest point in its postwar history.

10. These figures are from the author's data file for 1945-1979, and include willful abstentions as well as votes in defiance of the whips. Divisions that carry the three-line whip are an important test of loyalty because pairing is usually not permitted. The fact that cross-voting by Labour MPs has been increasing in recent years can also be seen by an examination of the division lists given in Norton (1975, 1980).

11. The listing of the rebuffs to the Party leaders during the past fifteen years presents only a partial image of the opposition. In a good number of instances, the spokesmen for the NEC accepted hostile resolutions rather than allowing them to proceed to votes which

TABLE 1
Conference Vote Against Party Leaders, 1946-1978

Resolution and Sponsor	Subject	Vote	Citation
ATTLEE GOVERNMENT			
1946: CLP	Government publicity	Hand	128, 131
TU	Public relations machinery	Hand	129, 131
CLP	Agricultural policy	Hand	182, 184
TU	Education	Hand	191, 195
1947: Comp., CLP	Tied cottages	50.1%	125-6, 127
Comp., CLP	Equal pay for women	79.4	157-8, 159
1948: Coop.	Subsidies on food and clothing	Hand	150-1, 152
TU	Tied cottages	Hand	212-3, 214
1949: None	---	-	-
1950: TU*	Food distribution	Hand	154-5, 157
OPPOSITION			
1952: Comp., TU	Tied cottages	Hand	178, 179
1953: None	---	-	-
1954: None	---	-	-
1955: None	---	-	-
1956: None	---	-	-
1957: None	---	-	-
1958: None	---	-	-
1960: 33, TU*	Nuclear defense	53.3	176, 202
60, TU*	Nuclear defense	50.3	178, 202
12, TU	Nuclear defense	52.6	181-2, 202
Policy, NEC	Nuclear defense	52.3	202
1961: 278, TU	Training of German troops in Britain	56.4	175, 194
Comp. 20, TU	Polaris bases	56.9	178, 194
1962: None	---	-	-
1963: None	---	-	-
WILSON GOVERNMENT			
1965: None	---	-	-
1966: Emerg. 2, TU*	Unemployment	51.9	228-9, 248
Comp. 13, TU*	Defense expenditures	54.2	249-51, 273
Comp. 34, TU	Vietnam	59.3	255-7, 273

(Continued)

TABLE 1 (Continued)

Resolution and Sponsor	Subject	Vote	Citation
WILSON GOVERNMENT (Continued)			
1967: Comp. 29, CLP	Incomes and price controls	51.9	163-4, 201
108, CLP	Economic development of regions	Hand	177-8, 201
Comp. 28, CLP	Vietnam	51.1	223-5, 236
Comp. 20, CLP	Military seizure in Greece	52.2	229-30, 236
1968: Comp. 22, TU*	Wage restrictions	81.9	122-4, 153
NEC Report	Fuel policy: coal mining	59.2	278-9, 283
Comp. 36, CLP	Rhodesia	55.0	287-9, 292
Amdmt., Comp. 20, CLP	Trades Union Congress economic policy	54.7	293-7, 299
Comp. 45, CLP	Charges for drug prescriptions	Hand	302-3, 307
254, CLP	Social security benefits	Hand	309, 312
1969: Comp. 36, CLP	Trades Union Congress economic policy	39.6	235-7, 267
OPPOSITION			
1970: Comp. 16, CLP	Superiority of Conference decisions	52.4	180-1, 185
Comp. 19, CLP	Incomes policy	52.4	214-6, 229
Comp. 11, TU	Business mergers	61.4	218-20, 229
1971: Comp. 33, CLP	Public ownership: banking and insurance	62.6	298-300, 307
Comp. 34, CLP	Public ownership: motor insurance	58.9	300-2, 307
1972: Comp. 37, TU*	Finance of housing	80.7	136-164
Comp. 32, CLP	Public ownership: decisive parts of economy	58.4	178-80, 193
1973: Comp. 26, TU	Public ownership: transport	Hand	148-150
Comp. 12, TU	Nuclear weapons/military expenditures	56.3	301-2, 312
WILSON/CALLAGHAN GOVERNMENTS			
1974: Emerg. 16, CLP	Common Market	51.4	251-2, 260
1975: Comp. 42, CLP	Housing	Hand	128-30, 147
Comp. 5, CLP	Social services in New Towns	Hand	135-6, 147
Comp. 27, TU	Import controls	Hand	155-6, 167
Comp. 33, CLP	Education	Hand	170-1, 175
Comp. 30, TU*	National Health Service	Hand	235-6, 245
Comp. 39, TU*	Increased pensions	Hand	249-50, 261
Comp. 40, CLP	Care of disabled persons	Hand	324-5, 330

TABLE 1 (Continued)

Resolution and Sponsor	Subject	Vote	Citation
WILSON/CALLAGHAN GOVERNMENTS (Continued)			
1976: Comp. 26, TU*	Cuts in social services	Hand	161-2, 181
Comp. 33, Coop	Housing	Hand	225-7, 239
Comp. 34, CLP	Housing	Hand	228-30, 239
Comp. 40, CLP	Sale of council houses	Hand	231-2, 239
Comp. 30, TU	National Health Service	Hand	255-8, 269
Comp. 35, CLP	Child benefits	Hand	259-61, 269
Comp. 39, TU	Care of disabled persons	Hand	298-303
1977: 266, CLP	Rhodesia	Hand	304-5, 308
320, CLP	Councillor penalties, Housing Finance Act	Hand	347-8, 349
1978: Comp. 41, CLP	National Health Service	Hand	186-7, 201
Comp. 37, CLP	Wage restraint	67.6	214-5, 230
Comp. 38, CLP	Wage restraint	56.4	216-7, 230
252, CLP	State subsidies to public schools	Hand	286-7, 297

Abbreviations: CLP, constituency Labour party; TU, trade union (*indicates among the ten largest); Coop., cooperative society; Comp., composite resolution. The page numbers cited are from the relevant *Annual Conference Report*. Omitted from this list are the defeats on organizational matters. Hand votes are not counted.

The issues that have brought the external units and the Party leaders into sharp conflict since 1966 may be grouped into four categories: (1) national defense and foreign policy (questions that have traditionally generated sparks within the Labour movement); (2) cuts in expenditures for the social services; (3) Britain's entry into the Common Market; and (4) economic issues, including government interference in the processes of collective bargaining. Some of these issues, of course, are interrelated. Curtailment of

were bound to result in the defeat of the leadership. This happened at the 1968 Conference, for example, when the NEC accepted censurious resolutions on prescription charges and on the sale of arms to Nigeria (see Annual Conference Report, 1968: 302-307, 260-265). A resolution at the 1975 Conference warning the Labour Government that it must remain faithful to its election pledges was accepted by none other than the Deputy Leader of the Party (see Annual Conference Report, 1975: 311-315). Again at the 1978 Conference, the NEC spokesman accepted a resolution on the economy that was clearly antithetical to the policies the Government was attempting to carry out (Annual Conference Report, 1978: 209, 226-230).

funds for public housing, for example, tends to reduce employment in the construction industry, and military expenditures resulting from foreign policy commitments are often viewed as a diversion of public resources from the social services. That the Labour Government had violated its election pledges has been a consistent theme in the speeches of delegates who proposed and seconded the censorious resolutions.

One of the crucial issues that has split both the parliamentary group and the mass organization is the Common Market, and it is another illustration of what happens when the two wings get out of step.[12] The 1971 Conference voted overwhelmingly against Britain's entrance into the European Community on the terms that had been negotiated by the Conservative Government. About *two weeks* later, however, when the issue was being considered in the House of Commons, 69 Labour members defied the whip and voted with the Tories, while 20 more abstained.

Many activists in the mass organization regarded this behavior as a flagrant challenge of the Conference decision, and some conjectured that the Conservative government might have fallen if the Labour pro-Marketeers had refrained from violating discipline. The incident strengthened the hand of the ideologists because, as in the case of unilateralism, they now had the authority of the Conference behind them. The Conference spoke to the issue on several other occasions, but the Labour Cabinet was already caught in a web of commitments. After the Labour MPs had been returned to the opposition benches, the Conference in 1980 supported Britain's withdrawal from the Common Market by an overwhelming vote of 71%.

The chasm between the Party leaders and the mass organization was widened by a series of "pocketbook" issues, some of which involved the free collective bargaining prerogatives of the trade unionists. The 1963 Conference, with the reticent support of some of the unions, had approved the principle of an incomes policy. In the face of a succession of economic crises, the Labour Government introduced phases of statutory wage restraint. But

---

12. For documentation on the Common Market issue, see Annual Conference Report (1971: 114-144); *The Times* (October 29, 1971); Annual Conference Report (1974: 177, 251-252, 260); *The Times* (October 2, 1980).

as the restrictions grew more severe, opposition to the policy increased, both within the parliamentary caucus and among the trade unions outside.

By 1968, the economic situation was complicated by industrial unrest which threatened to undermine the program of incomes control. The government responded by trying to introduce a bill (with three penal clauses included) to handle unofficial strikes and interunion jurisdictional disputes, even though the previous Conference had voted overwhelmingly for the repeal of wage controls and for the rejection of further legislation to curb trade union rights. The government's legislative plans provoked widespread resistance, which brought trade unionists who were usually loyal to the Party leadership into a joint campaign of opposition with the chronically discontented.

The Party leaders suffered what was perhaps their worst rebuff in 1978: the Conference delegates voted to support two resolutions against the holding of wage increases at a 5% norm, the major policy of the Callaghan Government. The mood of the Conference was displayed in the opening ritual when a representative of the Blackpool District Labour Party delivered his welcome to the delegates:

> "I am a leader of local workers in the town . . . so that I listen to workers and sometimes—not at the moment—they listen to me. I defended Phase 1, Phase 2 and I defended Phase 3. When it comes to Phase 4 there are some things you cannot defend. . . . I am standing here, speaking for ordinary constituencies, the ordinary workers in the trade union movement, and they are going to say, 'It is enough.' And they will get a following, and we shall be embarrassed if we are to go out in the party and try to substantiate such rubbish." [Annual Conference Report, 1978: 174].

But just as Wilson had ignored the Conference on some issues, Prime Minister Callaghan indicated that he would soldier on with his pay plan, despite the opposition of the Conference delegates.

STRUCTURAL CHANGE IN THE EXTERNAL PARTY

The increase in the number of successful rebellions against the Party leadership on the Conference floor in good part resulted from the Labour Government's having to assume responsibility for governing the nation under adverse circumstances, for the policies that were moved into focus served as a catalyst for dissident behavior. The hostile resolutions which emerged from the Conference were a clear indication that the traditional alliance between the PLP leaders and some of the large trade unions had broken down; the challenges to official policies could not have prevailed without backing from some of the strong union delegations.

But these issues were interacting with some structural changes which were taking place within the component units of the mass organizations and which noticeably altered the alignment of forces at the Conference.[13] Several unions had had a turnover of leadership owing to deaths and retirements, and in two of the larger unions (the Transport and General Workers' Union and the Amalgamated Union of Engineering and Foundry Workers), the new leaders were activists of left-wing proclivity. Besides that, the orthodox unions in declining industries suffered a downturn in membership which reduced the size of their Conference delegations. In addition, the outlooks of other loyalist unions underwent change as they were absorbed, through amalgamation, into organizations of leftist inclination. Finally, the service unions and the white-collar unions, some of which were under the influence of militant leadership, were attracting new members at a fairly rapid rate. All of these developments tended to erode the political resources of the Party leaders in the external organization.

Even the orthodox trade union leaders have encountered difficulty in rendering sustained support to the Party high command. The policies of the Labour Government were unpopular among the shop stewards and the ordinary workers on the assembly line. As rebellious outlooks were spreading among the rank and file members, the officials of previously loyal unions could continue to defend some of the Party's enunciated policies only at the risk of their own jobs, and they had trouble holding their Conference delegations in control. Moreover, some of these trade unionists

13. See Minkin (1978: 121-125; 321-324, 342-350); *The Times* (January 6, 1978); *Daily Telegraph* (February 21, 1979). Minkin's treatment of trade union outlooks is thorough and cogent.

were genuinely disappointed by Labour's performance in office and were now ready to register their disaffection with their Conference ballots.

Under these circumstances, the ability of the parliamentary leaders to penetrate the external party so as to secure endorsement for even its most salient policies was severely limited. Some union officials who were usually steadfast in their loyalty were thrown into apprehensive coalition with the left-wing ideologists in both the parliamentary and the nonparliamentary wings of the movement, and they found themselves supporting such strategies as a mass lobby of MPs in protest against cuts in public expenditures (The Times, October 27 and November 17, 1976). As a result of this realignment, the leftist elements in the Party began to operate on a bigger political base, from which they could proclaim the sovereignty of the Conference. After Labour's defeat in 1979, the swing to the left was accelerated, perhaps as a reaction to the right-wing policies of the Thatcher Government.

The diminished influence of the Party leaders on trade union behavior is recorded not only in policy voting at the Conference, but also in the election of members to the National Executive Committee. Traditionally, the members of the trade union section of the NEC were a fortress of loyalty for the parliamentary leadership, but several of those selected since 1968 have been of left-wing persuasion. The same can be said of the representatives elected to the women's section of the NEC by Conference-wide (and hence trade union) vote; they used to be firm supporters of the Party leaders, but since 1972 all but one of them have been people with leftist views. Similarly, the Conference used to elect the Party Treasurer from the orthodox wing of the organization, but since 1972 the post has been awarded, with the help of some of the unions, to a left-wing MP.

These changes in NEC membership are in addition to the shift that occurred during the Bevanite era when the constituency parties began to elect dissident MPs to their section. Thus, the National Executive Committee, with the help of some large unions, had moved conspicuously toward the leftward end of the political continuum, as shown by the following data drawn at five-year intervals from the beginning of the Wilson regime:

	1964	1969	1974	1979
Percentage of Leftist NEC Members	29%	43	48	62

During the past fifteen years, then, the leaders of the Parliamentary Labour Party have lost much of the informal influence they were once able to wield over the external organization. In Conference voting, they can no longer count on the allegiance of a coalition of dominant unions, and they can no longer command a dependable majority on the National Executive Committee, even though nearly three-fourths of the members are MPs. Attempts to establish better liaison between the two power centers in the Party, through such devices as special meetings of the NEC and Cabinet Ministers, have generally been ineffective.[14] The mass organization is laying claim to its sovereignty and, with the traditional method for securing harmony no longer operative, the two authority structures face each other in an atmosphere of suspicion and conflict. The two horses are getting harder for the Party Leader to ride.

CHANGING ROLE OF THE NATIONAL EXECUTIVE COMMITTEE

With the changing lineup of forces at the Conference and the political complexion of the National Executive Committee taking on a leftist hue, the role of the NEC has been noticeably modified. Since this organ is considered to be the instrument of the Conference, the activists who are able to win the floor debates have begun to look to the NEC to take a strong stand against the parliamentary group, and even the Labour Government, on the crucial issues which divide them. The ideological enthusiasts on the Committee, of course, have been more than willing to respond to this assignment.

14. See, for example, *The Times* (May 20, 1976; October 20, 1976; October 28, 1976; February 24, 1977; July 3, 1978; December 11, 1978) and *The Guardian* (November 1, 1979).

In the halcyon days, the NEC members used their debating time at the Conference to protect the Party leaders and to defend official policy, especially on the important issues. But this is no longer the case in any consistent way. Their changing role can be detected in their "winding-up" speeches at the conclusion of the debates held during the period when their own government was in power. In 1969, for example, Ian Mikardo underlined the conflict between the NEC and the Ministry over the issue of prescription charges, pointing out that the Minister had paid little heed to the Conference resolution of the previous year, and he urged the delegates to pass the hostile statement (Annual Conference Report, 1969: 353-354).

More recent examples include:

1975: criticism of the Labour Government for curtailing the railway investment program and for failing to cut military expenditures (Annual Conference Report, 1975: 278, 323-324).

1976: condemnation of the Party leaders for some of their financial policies, for their failure to trim military disbursements, and for not taking "a blind bit of notice" of the NEC request involving direct elections for the European Parliament (Annual Conference Report, 1976: 179-181, 250-255, 350).

1977: criticism of the Labour Government for carrying out a deflationary economic policy, for deficiencies in industrial investment, for its attitude toward pensions, and for unemployment in the construction industry growing out of the curtailment of public expenditures (Annual Conference Report, 1977: 180-182, 236-237, 301-303).

1978: support for an agricultural policy that the Minister opposed and for a resolution criticizing the Government for complicity in breaking up UN economic sanctions on trade with Rhodesia; calling the Government to account for the withering of the death grant program, for not carrying out its housing policy, and for failing to redeem its election pledge on freedom of information (Annual Conference Report, 1978: 244, 255-556, 302-303, 368-369).

The NEC has begun to envision itself as the guardian of Conference decisions.

Before we can examine the more aggressive role that the National Executive Committee has taken in the drawing up of policy statements in recent years, we must first consider the part it has usually played in this activity. The Committee has always had constitutional authority to submit for discussion and action "resolutions and declarations" on matters of "programme, principles, and policies." According to the Party Constitution, however, no proposal can be included in the Party Programme unless it has been passed by the Conference by a two-thirds vote recorded by card balloting. As an election approaches, the NEC is to meet with the Cabinet or the Shadow Cabinet to determine which items from the Programme shall be included in the election platform (Labour Party Constitution, 1979: clauses V and VIII (2) (g)).

When the Party is in a steady state, the NEC's policy-preparing role is dwarfed by the penetration of that body by the parliamentary leadership. When Labour takes office, the Cabinet becomes the most important center for formulating policy, and the ministers' busy schedules often leave them with little time for drawn-out consultations aimed at assessing the moods of the Party faithful in the mass organization. Although the leaders have more extensive contacts with the external units when they move into opposition, even then they have usually had a strong influence on policy statements so long as they are not sharply divided among themselves.

The traditionally dominant role of the Party leaders in policy matters is discernible when the time comes for drafting the election platform. Tensions usually arise between those platform committee members who are strongly attached to doctrine and insist upon detailed policy commitments, and the top Party strategists who demand a relatively short, general statement which will attract rather than frighten the middle-of-the-road voters. Working under tight deadlines, the committee members feel pressure to reach agreement, and the Party Leader and his colleagues have customarily had a decisive voice in determining what issues should be emphasized and what should be excluded.

In the late 1960s, the National Executive Committee began to operate more independently of the parliamentary leadership in preparing policy statements for the Party to consider (Minkin, 1978: 296-339; Hatfield, 1978). One of the objectives of the left-wing faction was to develop a set of economic and social policies well enough in advance so that they would become the basis for future election platforms and would constitute an agenda for future Labour governments. The NEC—backed up by the Research Department at Transport House and operating through a myriad of committees, subcommittees, and working groups (with nearly 1000 people, including trade unionists and parliamentarians, serving on more than eighty units during the opposition years 1970-1974)—studied a variety of issues, drafted scores of working papers, and hammered out a number of important policy statements.

In general, the partisans of the left tended to take the initiative in this survey of issues; the people of right-wing sympathy were as a rule not quite so assiduous in their work and they gave less of a lead than their leftist colleagues, who managed to gain control of the key study groups. From these extensive discussions there eventually emerged two documents, *Labour's Programme 1973* and *Labour's Programme 1976,* which were comprehensive in scope and leftward in orientation. Both policy statements became a framework for resolutions that were passed by the Party Conference, and the 1976 document was officially approved by that body.

Needless to say, the results of the NEC's effort in laying the groundwork for policy failed to capture the enthusiasm of the Party leaders. Harold Wilson regarded the 1973 statement as an electoral liability, asserting that the committee responsible for drawing up the platform would "veto" some of the objectionable features (Hatfield, 1978: 196-211; The Times, January 11-12, 1974; Butler and Kavanagh, 1980: 144-153). Similarly, Callaghan took exception to certain parts of the 1976 document. Hence, the way was opened up for criticism that recent election platforms—and especially the 1979 document—watered down, glossed over, or omitted certain controversial issues, a good number of which had been endorsed by the Party Conference.

The suspicion that the Party leaders had manipulated the platform committee so as to avoid taking clear stands on issues on which the Conference had already committed the Party enraged many activists in the mass organization. In recent years, the Conference debates have been peppered with complaints about how certain decisions mandated by the Conference were either ignored or inadequately enunciated in the election platform. In the view of the delegates, the parliamentary leaders were disregarding the voice of the movement, not only in preparing the platform, but also in carrying out the business of government after they had entered office.

As we can surmise from Table 1, the substance of the indictment ranged widely: The Party leadership had defied the authority of the Conference by continuing to support American military action in Vietnam, by being more concerned about the balance of payments than with economic growth, by delaying the liquidation of commitments east of Suez, by retaining the charges on drug prescriptions and cutting back on other social services, by sticking to the policy of wage controls, by attempting the statutory regulation of unofficial strikes, and by not taking steps to pull Britain out of the Common Market.

The deep resentment of the Labour rank and file against the Party strategists for their lack of respect for Conference decisions can be seen in the flow of Conference resolutions on the subject.[15] Folk wisdom, reinforced by a few isolated studies, suggests that resolutions hostile to the leadership tend to come from Labour parties in "safe" Tory areas. (A "safe" constituency is defined as one in which the winning party has at least a 25% majority.) But this is not true of the protests that have been lodged against the Party leaders for their defiance of Conference mandates. Between 1971 and 1979, the constituency parties submitted a total of 40 resolutions urging the parliamentary leaders to abide by Conference decisions. That these protests were largely from the party faithful in Labour territory is shown by the indicated breakdown

---

15. Statistics on Conference resolutions used in this article have been compiled from the annual list of resolutions for period 1971-1980. They do not include amendments to the resolutions.

of local Labour parties as sources for hostile resolutions on the issue of Conference autonomy:

Resolutions	Parties with Labour MPs	Parties with Opposition MPs	Parties in Safe Labour Areas	Parties in Safe Tory Areas	N
Conference Autonomy	60%	40	25	10	(40)

Basically, of course, the issue involves conflicting theories of parliamentary representation. Jack Jones, the leader of the Transport and General Workers' Union, put the matter in a straightforward way at the 1970 Conference: "For too long the idea has been about that an MP was just a representative, and not a delegate" (Annual Conference Report, 1970: 176, 180-185). This view was echoed a year later by Hugh Scanlon, the head of the Amalgamated Union of Engineering Workers: "I hope that . . . there is a definite decision that decisions of Party Conference are binding on us all, and that includes every MP of this Party" (Report of a Special Conference of the Labour Party, 1971: 31). Harold Wilson, however, clearly expressed the attitude of the leadership at a Party Conference which had rebuffed him in six defeats, one of them (on his incomes policy) by an adverse vote of 82%: he was disposed to treat these decisions of censure as a "warning" to the PLP, but not as an "instruction."[16]

The changes in the leadership and structure of some of the trade unions has precipitated a decline in the penetrative capability of the Party high command to keep the mass organization under its control. Feeding into these structural changes, however, was a series of controversial issues which arose from the policies adopted by the Labour Government and which tended to persist over time. These developments have played into the hands of the ideological enthusiasts, tipping the fulcrum of power in the external party toward the dissident left. This shift in the balance of forces in the mass organization has been reflected in two ways: (1) by the Conference passing resolutions that were contrary to the wishes of the Party leaders, and (2) by the election of left-wing

16. Annual Conference Report (1968: 299). For Callaghan's position, see Annual Conference Report (1979: 228-229) and *Daily Telegraph* (August 15, 1979).

members of the National Executive Committee, which sees its role as one of defending the interests of the Conference rather than protecting the Party leadership and of initiating policy studies and statements independently of that leadership.

Tightening the Harness of the Parliamentary Horse

When the critics of the parliamentary leaders were successful in scoring victories on the Conference floor, they were understandably eager to convert their strength in the mass organization into power in the House of Commons. The feeling that some Labour MPs have "risen above the movement," acting contrary to the "wishes of the working class," has prompted many zealots and their recently persuaded allies to demand procedures for making the Party leaders and individual MPs more accountable. These procedures involve: (1) control over the renomination process, (2) control over the selection of the Party Leader, and (3) control over the writing of the election platform.

CONTROL OVER THE RENOMINATION PROCESS

The activists' most vigorous effort thus far has been aimed at getting rid of sitting members of parliament who, for one reason or another, have lost the support of party workers in their constituencies. As one Conference delegate expressed the idea, "If the Parliamentarians are not going to take note of the Conference, then let us make them take note of the constituencies" (Annual Conference Report, 1974: 173).

The Parliamentary Labour Party has always operated on the assumption that if its members are expected to obey the whips, they must be protected from erratic action by their local parties and/or from conspiracies by unrepresentative minorities which may have seized control of the constituency organizations. The traditional rules were designed to make it difficult for local parties to deny sitting MPs a chance to retain their seats.[17] They provided that in the case of incumbents, the machinery for selecting the candidate would ordinarily not be put into gear "until an election (was) imminent." This meant that there would hardly be enough time to go through the full-blown selection process, and except in the most unusual circumstances the incumbent was readopted. In his study of candidate selection for the eighteen-year period between 1946 and 1963, Ranney was able to identify only eight cases of local Labour parties that wanted to discard their MPs (Ranney, 1965: 182-183).

Since 1974, however, the Party has been plagued by readoption problems. In dramatic contrast with the situation described by Ranney, at least 29 constituency organizations indicated displeasure with their parliamentary representatives in the short five-year period between mid-1974 and the 1979 election, and nearly one-half of the MPs were either refused readoption or chose to retire.[18] More cases might have come to light had it not been for the fact that some parties concealed their discontent when they thought that an election would be called in the autumn of 1978.

The flareup of readoption cases is an outgrowth of several factors. In some cases, the local parties were weak and vulnerable to takeover by groups that had organized against their MPs. In a constituency organization where the membership had declined and the old-timers were absorbed in borough council work to the neglect of their party responsibilities, dissidents were able to push their resolutions through the general committee which was small and had often poorly attended meetings. The lineup of political

17. See "Model Rules for Constituency Labour Parties," Annual Conference Report (1974) Appendix 3, pp. 348-349, Clause XIV, 7.
18. Intraparty squabbles at the local level are often hidden from public view, and it is difficult to secure information except for the most serious disputes. The information presented in this article has been gathered from interviews and from newspaper accounts during the period 1974-1979. Dick Taverne (Lincoln) ran into trouble in his constituency party because of his vote on the Common Market, but his case is not included in these calculations since it occurred prior to 1974. It is interesting to note that some Conservative MPs have also been experiencing difficulty with their local organizations (see, for example, The Times, March 3, 1970; March 11, 1971; September 21, 1977; The Guardian, January 14, 1981). Backbench rebellions in the Conservative Party have also been increasing in recent years (see Norton, 1978).

forces in some local parties was affected by demographic change as young people in middle-class occupations or trade unionists in white-collar unions moved into the district to take advantage of lower rents.[19] In more than a few instances the move to reject a sitting MP was spearheaded by politically restless students or young teachers who linked arms with militant trade unionists (The Times, November 27 and 29, 1976). The decline in the number of full-time party agents (from a peak of nearly 300 in the early 1950s to only 81 in 1979) made the constituency units open to assault, since they lacked continuity in organization and management (Williams, 1951: 64; Annual Conference Report, 1979: 22).

One reason for the increased militancy in some constituency parties was the decision of the National Executive Committee to abandon the list of proscribed organizations: This action made it somewhat easier for extremist elements to become involved in the affairs of the local parties (Annual Conference Report, 1973: 11). Amid charges that Trotskyists were infiltrating Labour's local units, the National Agent in 1975 investigated their activities and submitted his report to the NEC. Although both Wilson and Callaghan warned of the danger of subtle "entryism" by subversive groups, the Party has thus far failed to take appropriate action.[20]

Another factor that has influenced the incidence of readoption cases is the changed attitude of the National Executive Committee. In earlier times, its members were concerned about protecting the candidature of loyal MPs who had fallen under attack by local activists. The National Agent was usually able to smooth out disagreements of this sort by informal mediation, and few members were denied another try for their seats. Now, however, the NEC handles the readoption cases differently. The disputes are brought before that body officially, and, standing aside from

19. This is apparently what happened in the local party at Newham Northeast, which ousted Reginald Prentice, a Cabinet minister. For early accounts of this case, see issues of The Economist for July 1975.

20. See The Times (November 10, 1975; December 12, 1975; November 30, 1976; December 2, 1976); and The Guardian (January 8-9, 1980; January 24, 1980). For important Conference speeches on the subject, see Annual Conference Report (1975: 187; 1976: 193; 1979: 191-192).

the substantive issues, it merely inquires whether the procedural rules have been violated. In other words, the NEC is less willing to press for reversal of a local party's decision to unload its MP, thereby weakening the protection of parliamentary members who have been faithful to the whip.

Why would the members of a constituency party be interested in denying renomination to their member of parliament? Some local units wanted to shake off their MPs for "personal" reasons: they were "getting too old," they were not diligent in their House of Commons work, or they were neglecting their constituencies. Some MPs had created discontent in their local organizations, and dissident groups sought to exploit it and make an opening for a more suitable replacement. In some parties the difficulties eventually melted away, but in others the struggle between the left and the right was sharpened.

One of the main complaints that constituency parties had against their parliamentary representatives was the views they held on certain political issues. Some MPs were attacked for supporting the Labour Government on policies the local activists considered to be "unsocialist." A frequent cause of tension was an MP's support for Britain's entry into the Common Market. In the 29 constituency parties in which the parliamentary members experienced difficulty between 1974 and 1979, no fewer than 18 of the MPs (62%) were known to be advocates of Britain joining the European Community, and some of them had defied the whips on the issue.

On December 6, 1976, in a speech at Batley, Yorkshire (The Times, December 6), Wilson pointed out the problem that local parties were creating when they judged their parliamentarians on the basis of policy stands:

> Respected MPs, enjoying the endorsement of a democratic electorate, are now the target for no reason other than that they vote consistently in favor of the Labour government they were elected to support, vote consistently for the policies of the manifesto on which they received that endorsement.

In an attempt to make their MPs accountable to the "party organization which was instrumental to [their] selection and election,"[21] some local parties began to exact accountability pledges from potential candidates at the time of their selection.[22] A demand for accountability was also made by the Yorkshire area council of the Mineworkers' Union, whose guidelines for parliamentary behavior required that its sponsored MPs promise not to vote against union policy on any major issue.[23]

The experience derived from attempts to jettison individual members of parliament led to demands that they should be subjected to institutionalized scrutiny at mid-term. Such a strategy would result in a broader sweep of change rather than tackling one MP at a time through the ad hoc process. Between 1971 and 1980, the constituency parties submitted a total of 139 resolutions to the Conference calling for a full selection process to be instituted by each local party during the lifetime of a parliament, with the sitting member being placed on the short list automatically.[24] Again, this was not agitation entirely from Labour parties in safe Tory areas: 47% of the resolutions came from constituencies where Labour held the seats, and 53% of them originated in areas held by the opposition. Pressures for the reselection scheme mounted over time, reaching a peak at the 1977 Conference, when one resolution for mandatory reselection meetings was sponsored by 67 local parties (Annual Conference Agenda, 1977: 15).

In response to Conference pressure, the National Executive Committee formed a working party to study the issue (The National Executive Committee Report, 1978: 172-178, Appendix I). Although a vocal minority favored the system under which a full selection meeting was mandatory, the majority of the members of the study group supported a compromise solution.

21. The quotation is from the left-wing Campaign for Labour Democracy, reported in *The Times* (July 8, 1975).

22. For cases involving Lambeth, Vauxhall, and Kensington and Chelsea, see *The Times* (July 28, 1976· August 6, 1976; August 10, 1976, March 15, 1977; April 5, 1977). The NEC's Organization Committee later ruled that an effort to secure such guarantees was constitutionally improper.

23. *The Times* (June 26, 1975; June 30, 1975; July 21, 1975; October 23, 1975). Later, the Committee on Privileges in the House of Commons ruled that such action constituted an invasion of parliamentary privilege, and the Yorkshire area resolution was nullified by the authorities in the national union. For the accountability outlook of the London Cooperative Society, see *The Times* (July 2, 1975).

24. An early and "model" resolution was presented at the 1974 Conference (see Annual Conference Report, 1974: 170-182).

Under their arrangement, a local party was required to convene a special meeting of its general committee within a period of 18 to 36 months after the election. If the delegates at this meeting were satisfied with their MP's performance, the full selection procedure would not be invoked. But if the decision was unfavorable, the machinery for selecting a candidate would be set in motion, with the MP's name appearing on the list of potential nominees. At the 1978 Conference, the delegates rejected the proposal for a mandatory selection process by a close vote and then adopted the proposal of the working party by a much wider margin (Annual Conference Report, 1978: 271-282). But this decision did not end the matter. At the 1979 Conference, the NEC waived the rules to permit the issue to be debated again, and this time the plan for mandatory reselection was adopted by 57% of the vote (Annual Conference Report 1979: 262-271). This decision was reaffirmed by the 1980 Conference when the delegates, in a reduced vote of 53%, adopted the necessary amendment to the Party Constitution.

No longer is it possible for a Labour member of parliament to ask for readoption on the eve of an election when no competitors are available. The word "mandatory" is significant in the new procedure. Had the earlier compromise proposal become the rule, the burden would have rested upon the constituency party to demonstrate the need for changing its MP. Under the mandatory system, however, the burden of justification is shifted to the sitting member against the groups that are pressing for removal, and this must be done while competitors are waiting in the wings. The mass organization now has a bridle for keeping its parliamentary contingent in tighter rein.

CONTROL OVER THE SELECTION OF THE PARTY LEADER

The Party Leader has traditionally been elected by the members of the Parliamentary Labour Party, and, through custom, has come to be regarded as the Leader of the entire Party. In recent years, however, the activists who have sought to make the MPs more accountable have also attempted to curtail the power of the PLP by having the Party Leader chosen by a broader constituency.[25] In the period from 1971 to 1980, the constituency parties submitted a total of 48 resolutions to the various Conferences calling for a change in the selection of the Leader, and 34 of these appeared in 1979 and 1980. As with the other issues, this sentiment was not confined to Labour parties in hopelessly Conservative territories; about 40% of the resolutions were authored by parties with sitting Labour MPs.

The issue came to a boil at the 1979 Conference, when the delegates voted on a proposal to have the Leader chosen by an "electoral college." However, some of the trade unions that had voted for the mandatory reselection of MPs did not warm up to this plan, and the proposal was defeated by a 57% vote (Annual Conference Report, 1979: 251-262, 271; The Guardian, October 3, 1979). This decision was reversed at the 1980 Conference by a narrow vote of 50.7% when the delegates decided to have the Leader chosen by an electoral college made up of Labour MPs, representatives from the trade unions, and activists from the constituency parties, although after several attempts they could not agree on a voting formula.

A final decision on this matter was reached at a special Conference held in January 1981, and the delegates voted to give 40% of the voting strength to the unions, 30% to the Labour MPs, and 30% to the constituency parties.[26] Some of the larger unions wanted the MPs to have the strongest voice in the electoral college, but a mix-up in their tactical voting played into the hands of those who wanted to reduce the influence of the PLP. The engineering union, for example, wanted the MPs to have 75% of the votes in the selection of the Leader, but the union abstained in the balloting for other options. This victory for the left was too much for some moderate MPs, and a few days later about ten of them announced the formation of a breakaway party.

25. The case for changing the procedures for selecting the Party Leader is presented in Coates (1977).
26. See *The Times* (January 26, 1981). In examining the resolutions submitted to the Special Conference in 1981, we can see that the sentiment for drastically revising the leadership selection procedures was not monopolized by dissident Labour parties

CONTROL OVER THE WRITING OF
THE ELECTION PLATFORM

Tensions between the NEC representatives on the platform committee and the parliamentary leaders had emerged during the drafting of the election statements for previous elections, but the strains were particularly severe as they sat down to prepare the 1979 platform.[27] Most of the NEC members of the drafting committee insisted that the document be framed around Conference decisions, but the Prime Minister and his fellow-strategists resisted this approach. They were painfully aware that some Conference decisions ran counter to the policies of their Government, and they regarded others as serious election liabilities. Although Callaghan and his colleagues made a few concessions to the left, the pressure of time resulted in other NEC proposals being diluted and some being excluded from the document. The elaborate work done by the NEC appeared to have had only marginal effect.

Labour's defeat at the polls, on what some activists regarded as a Cabinet-butchered platform, did little to quench the fires of

operating in Conservative territory. The weighted vote options in favor of the unions and the constituency parties drew considerable support from Labour parties with sitting MPs.

	Constituency Parties with Labour MPs	Constituency Parties with Opposition MPs	Safe Labour Areas	Safe Tory Areas	N
Weighted in favor of PLP	10.2%	12.4	7.1	19.2	(37)
Weighted in favor of Trade Unions	31.4	27.6	23.8	24.7	(94)
Weighted in favor of Constituency Parties	7.3	4.3	4.8	1.4	(18)
Equal Weighting among the three groups	24.1	30.8	23.8	27.4	(90)
Election by Party Members	24.8	21.6	38.1	24.7	(74)
Miscellaneous	2.2	3.2	2.4	2.7	(9)
	(N=137)	(N=185)	(N=42)	(N=73)	

SOURCE: *Agenda for the Special Rules Revision Conference,* January 24, 1981, London: The Labour Party, 1981.

27. See *Daily Telegraph* (December 11, 1978; April 7, 1970); *The Times* (July 3, 1978);

discent at the 1979 Conference six months later. The constituency parties submitted 26 resolutions to the assembly urging that the framing of the platform be placed entirely in the hands of the National Executive Committee. About 42% of these resolutions were incubated in local parties with sitting Labour MPs.

Callaghan regarded the question of platform authorship as even more serious than the reselection of MPs and the method of choosing the Party Leader, and he hoped that the trade unions would come to his rescue. But they failed to respond with enough votes, and by a narrow tally of 50.3%, the Conference committed the Party to the principle of having the National Executive Committee take over the writing of the platform (Annual Conference Report, 1979: 275-282). This decision, however, was reversed a year later by another close vote of 50.8%. Under the Party rules, the Conference cannot discuss the matter again for three more years, unless the NEC decides to waive the rules as it did on the question of reselecting the MPs. With such close votes on the issue of the drafting of the election statement, it is probable that the Conference will decide to give this responsibility to the NEC, which will then be in a position to write a militant platform for the next election, if the present Conservative regime is able to hang on until 1984.

The Problem of The Horses Out of Step

The growing power of the mass organization has important implications for the electoral success of the Labour Party and for the operation of its parliamentary wing in the House of Commons. The choosing of the Leader through an electoral college opens up the possibility that a Labour Prime Minister who pursues necessary but unpopular policies may be removed from his position as Leader of the Labour Party by a coalition of rebellious trade unionists and constituency activists, in collaboration with dissident Labour MPs. The monarch might then be faced with the

---

The Guardian (August 15, 1979; November 1, 1979); Butler and Kavanagh (1980: 144-153); and Layton-Henry (1979: 435-440).

problem of determining who can command a majority in the House of Commons, and the choice may not coincide with that of the electoral college. The shifting moods of the mass organization are likely to be reflected in an instability of leadership, and it is possible that from time to time the mantle will fall on a stalwart from the left whose views are hopelessly out of line with the attitudes of the mainstream of British voters.

It is somewhat easier to predict the outcome of having the National Executive Committee become the sole author of the election platform, especially if its left-wing complexion remains unchanged. We can anticipate platforms that are more extreme in substance. This situation can create survival problems for a party in which the outlooks of most activists and many parliamentarians are already more out of tune with the views of their voting clientele than is the case with the Conservatives.

Perhaps more interesting from a political science perspective is the effect of the mandatory reselection of incumbent MPs upon the operation of the Labour Party in the House of Commons. Labour members of parliament are the servants of several masters. They are expected to remain loyal to their parliamentary leaders and obey the whips; to represent *all* of the people in their constituencies; to respond to the wishes of their local party activists; to be attentive to the interests of the affiliated organization sponsoring their candidacies; and to pay some heed to Conference decisions. Occupying a role made up of so many requirements, the Labour MP is bound to be cross-pressured when the masters to whom allegiance is owed issue conflicting commands.

Until local parties began to put their MPs on the carpet, the conventions of the House of Commons and the norms of the Labour Party dictated that, under ordinary circumstances, the member's obligation to the leadership be given priority over the other expectations, providing protection from pressures exerted by the local party or by the Conference. But now the activists in a constituency organization have an easier, institutionalized procedure for discarding their MPs if they dislike their voting records or for some other reason consider them unworthy. The role expectations, in other words, emanate from two sources rather than one, and the demands of the local activists are likely at times to be incompatible with those of the parliamentary leadership.

The bifurcation of power relationships will probably encourage an MP to be more sensitive to the views of the local activists. Instead of coming to the general committee meeting in the cloak of a "hero," delivering a short address, and then catching the next train to London, the MP will have to spend more time bolstering political fences and developing closer ties with the people who do the doorstep work and have the determining voice in readoption, and will certainly have to devote more attention to the "education" of the young militants in the party, who are eager to press onward to the "new social order" and are impatient with the detours of the pragmatists.

The important question is this: What will the MP do when the PLP leaders and the constituency activists pull in different directions? Our political science "knowledge" prompts the speculation that the MPs' first loyalty will be to the constituency parties which were responsible for getting them to Westminster and which now have the power to deny candidature. The increased concern of a legislative representative for the local constituency is bound to erode party discipline in any parliamentary chamber, and is likely, therefore, to inject a measure of instability into the system. Party discipline, for example, is an important ingredient of stability in both two-party and multiparty systems.

If there is a shift in primary allegiance from the parliamentary leadership to the local party, Labour's discipline in the House of Commons will obviously be affected. Already there are signs that the authority of the Party's high command is being undermined. Even at the time when the Callaghan Government desperately needed support because it had to carry on without a clear majority, the whips reported that some MPs, whose local parties were urging them to abstain on certain unpopular measures, had become unreliable at division time. Not too long ago, the whips could say to a rebel: "Stick with the team or we will report you to your local party," and the threat would have had an effect. But now the dissidents *want* their rebellious behavior reported to their home organizations!

In their struggle to gain authority to reselect the members of parliament, the organization that headed the drive, as well as some constituency parties, have contended either explicitly or implicitly that an MP should be primarily a delegate who is accountable to, or even subject to the direction of, the local party being represented. The inference is strong that a parliamentary representative is no longer a *trustee* who must be concerned with the "common good," as so many of them now define their role, but is a *delegate* who is obligated to vote according to constituency directive. In the emotional, drawn-out debates, the statement was often made that the parliamentary member is to be "responsible to the local party." For many activists, this means the general committee of the party, which is the decision-making organ.

Making an MP accountable to the local general committee poses some sticky problems for the theorist of representation. First of all, the committee is usually very small and cannot be seen as a good sample of the inhabitants of a constituency, of the Labour voters in the area, or even of the people who have bothered to sign up for Labour Party membership. The decision makers in the local party are those whose threshold of boredom is so low that they attend the meetings of the general committee, and often they are the people whose sense of humor is displaced by their sense of mission. Besides that, many general committees are more unstable than they used to be, and their composition, as well as their political coloration, sometimes changes rapidly. Fluctuations in committee membership may make it difficult for an MP to satisfy a moderate general committee one year and a more leftist one the next. Finally, the small size of a general committee, the spotty attendance record, and its changing makeup facilitate control by organized pressure groups or by militants who may be out of step with the interests and feelings of ordinary Labour people in the constituency.

In sum, then, the opponents of the parliamentary leadership have managed to fasten their control over Labour's external organization, turning the Conference into an indefatigable critic, rendering the MPs accountable to what can be a thin, evanescent majority of activists in the constituency parties, snatching the selection of the Party Leader from the hands of the parliamentary caucus, and threatening to give the NEC sole responsibility for drafting the election platform. These developments pose a threat to the traditional disciplined solidarity of the Labour Party in the House of Commons. For the leader of the Party, the changes in the configuration of power will make it increasingly difficult to straddle the two horses. But for the political scientist, the "circus" should provide rich opportunities for the study of coalition building.

Since this essay has focused upon the British Labour Party, the author is open to the charge that the case selected for examination is idiosyncratic. It is his contention, however, that the outline of this study has wider applicability and can be refined by the addition of other cases. Often the assumption is made that the parliamentary party, under the control of its leaders, has a relatively free hand in framing policy. But this assumption needs to be checked by empirical investigation. Authors of books on particular parties, as well as political journalists, describe factional disputes, and their accounts indicate that the cleavages within the parliamentary group are carried over into the extraparliamentary units. The author's preliminary reading suggests an examination of such organizations as the Australian Labour Party, the French Socialist Party, the Labour Party in Ireland, the Israeli Labor Party, the New Zealand Labour Party, and the Swedish Social Democratic Party.[28]

The political science literature embraces a good number of elite studies and much has been written about mass political behavior. Studies that seek to bridge the two levels, however, are less plentiful. This essay is an attempt to deal with the linkages between the parliamentary elite and the activists in the external party

28. Australian Labour Party: Crisp (1961: Chapter 6), Overacker (1952: Chapters 5 and 7), Stevens and Weller (1976), Starr (1978: Ch. 3). French Socialist Party: Codding and Safran (1979), Micaud (1956: 134-138), Simmons (1970: Chapters 4, 5, and 11-13). Labor Party in Ireland: Lyons (1951), Moss (1933: 74-79). Israeli Labour Party: Aronoff (1977). New Zealand Labour Party: Kelson (1964: Chapters 3 and 4), Milne (1966: Chapters 6 and 7), Overacker (1957: 27). Swedish Social Democratic Party: Bock and Berglund (1978). (The author is indebted to Robert Kvavik for this latter reference.)

organization; in other words, it examines issue-oriented factional behavior within a defined organizational setting.

Before the utility of the framework employed in this study can be demonstrated, more in-depth research has to be directed toward this type of linkage in political parties in other countries. In structuring the exploration, investigators might consider placing the following items on their research agendas: a typing of the ideology that the party professes; the nature of the cleavage within the parliamentary group; the structure of the mass organization, the locus of power within it, and its relationship to the parliamentary caucus; the degree of penetration of the external party by the party leaders and the techniques employed in the penetration; the changing relationships between the parliamentary group and the mass organization when the party comes to power and when it returns to an opposition role; changes in the structure of the external party and their impact upon the distribution of power within the external units, as well as upon the penetrative influence of the parliamentary leadership; the effect of emotional and "bread and butter" issues upon the cleavages within the parliamentary caucus and upon the activists in the mass organization and, through them, upon the structure of the mass organization; and the differences between the structures and the flow of developments within them in left-wing and right-wing parties. Research of this type will bring the analysis of particular species of factionalism into an organizational context and may encourage exciting theorizing about political parties.

Date of receipt of final manuscript: April 2, 1981

REFERENCES

ARONOFF, M. J. (1977) Power and Ritual in the Israel Labor Party: A Study in Political Anthropology. Amsterdam: Van Gorcum.

BOCK, P.-E. and S. BERGLUND (1978) Det Svenska partiväsendet. Stockholm: Almquist and Wiksell Folag.

BUTLER, D. and D. KAVANAGH (1980) The British General Election of 1979. London: Macmillan.

COATES, K. (1977) Democracy in the Labour Party. Nottingham: Spokesman.

CODDING, G. M., Jr. and W. SAFRAN (1979) Ideology and Politics: The Socialist Party in France. Boulder, CO: Westview.

CRISP, L. F. (1961) Australian National Government. London: Longmans.

CROSLAND, A. (1960) Can Labour Lose? Fabian Society Tract 324. London: Fabian Society.

—— (1953) "The transition from capitalism," pp. 33-68 in R.H.S. Crossman (ed.) New Fabian Essays. London: Turnstile Press.

DUVERGER, M. (1954) Political Parties: Their Organization and Activity in the Modern State. New York: John Wiley.

HATFIELD, M. (1978) The House the Left Built: Inside Labour Policy-Making, 1970-1975. London: Victor Gollancz.

—— (1973) "Mr. Wilson and his circus." The Times (London) June 1.

KELSON, R. N. (1964) The Private Member of Parliament and the Formation of Public Policy: A New Zealand Case Study. Toronto: Univ. of Toronto Press.

The Labour Party (1945-1981) Annual Conference Report. London: The Labour Party.

—— (1981) Agenda for the Special Rules Revision Conference, January 24, London: The Labour Party.

—— (1979) Party Constitution and Standing Orders. London: The Labour Party.

—— (1978) Report of the National Executive Committee of the Labour Party. London: The Labour Party.

—— (1977) Agenda for the Seventy-Sixth Annual Conference of the Labour Party. London: The Labour Party.

—— (1971) Labour and the Common Market: Report of a Special Conference of the Labour Party, July 17. London: The Labour Party.

LAYTON-HENRY, Z. (1979) "Reforming the Labour Party." Political Q. 50, 4 (October-December): 435-444.

LYONS, F.S.L. (1951) The Irish Parliamentary Party, 1890-1910. London: Faber and Faber.

McKENZIE, R. T. (1963) British Political Parties: The Distribution of Power Within the Conservative and Labour Parties. New York: Praeger.

MICAUD, C. A. (1956) "French political parties: ideological myths and social realities," pp. 106-154 in S. Neumann (ed.) Modern Political Parties. Chicago: Univ. of Chicago Press.

MILNE, R. S. (1966) Political Parties in New Zealand. Oxford: Clarendon.

MINKIN, L. (1978) The Labour Party Conference: A Study of the Politics of Intra-Party Democracy. London: Allen Lane.

MOSS, W. (1933) Political Parties in the Irish Free State. New York: Columbia Univ. Press.

NORTON, P. (1980) Dissension in the House of Commons, 1974-1979. Oxford: Clarendon.

—— (1978) Conservative Dissidents: Dissent Within the Parliamentary Conservative Party, 1970-1974. London: Maurice Temple Smith.

—— (1975) Dissension in the House of Commons: Intra-Party Dissent in the House of Commons Division Lobbies, 1945-1974. London: Macmillan.

OVERACKER, L. (1957) "The British and New Zealand Labour Parties: a comparison, part 2: today." Political Sci. 9, 2 (September): 15-31.

—— (1952) The Australian Party System. New Haven: Yale Univ. Press.

PHILLIPS, M. (1960) Constitution of the Labour Party. London: The Labour Party.

RANNEY, A. (1965) Pathways to Parliament: Candidate Selection in Britain. Madison: Univ. of Wisconsin Press.

SIMMONS, H. G. (1970) French Socialists in Search of a Role, 1956-1967. Ithaca, NY: Cornell Univ. Press.

STARR, G., K. RICHMOND and G. MADDOX (1978) Political Parties in Australia. Richmond, Victoria, Australia: Heinemann Educational.

STEVENS, B. and P. WELLER [eds.] (1976) The Australian Labor Party and Federal Politics: A Documentary Survey. Carlton, Victoria, Australia: Melbourne Univ. Press.

THOMPSON, J. D. (1967) Organizations in Action: Social Science Bases of Administrative Theory. New York: McGraw-Hill.

TURNER, J. E. (1978) Labour's Doorstep Politics in London. Minneapolis: Univ. of Minnesota Press.

WILLIAMS, A. L. (1951) "Lessons of the 1950 General Election." Labour Organiser 30, 349 (April): 64-65.

Peacemaking and Vested Interests

International Economic Transactions

RUTH W. ARAD
SEEV HIRSCH
Faculty of Management
Tel Aviv University

Two neighboring countries which have been at war with each other decide to make peace. Their governments undertake to allow their citizens to engage in trade and other economic transactions. This article considers the impact of different bilateral transactions on the welfare of producers and consumers in the two countries and hence on their attitude toward peace. Distinction is made between the effects of different kinds of transactions, including those involving existing and new trade as well as existing and new productions. Special reference is made to the recent Egyptian-Israeli peace effort.

Introduction

The peace treaty concluded between Israel and Egypt in March 1979 is no more than a milestone along a broader process of gradual reconciliation between two previously warring nations. This process of arriving at a stable peace will presumably go on, but it will probably be agonizingly slow and arduous. The effort will require supreme statesmanship on the part of all concerned, not only in successfully resolving those political issues that are still subjects of contention between the two nations, but also in attenuating the antagonisms which permeated their long and tragic conflict.

AUTHORS' NOTE: This article is based on research funded by the Tel Aviv University Research Project on Peace. The authors wish to thank Uzi Arad, Alfred Tovias, anonymous referees, and the editors of this journal for helpful comments and suggestions.

INTERNATIONAL STUDIES QUARTERLY, Vol. 25 No. 3, September 1981 439-468
© 1981 I.S.A.

There were many underlying causes of the conflict between Egypt and Israel, all political and strategic in nature, rather than economic. But to say that economic issues played a relatively minor role in the history of the conflict is not to say that they will remain modest in significance throughout the process of its resolution. Actually, economic considerations have been major determinants in both nations' crucial decisions to venture along the road to peace. Egypt's and Israel's internal economic predicaments undoubtedly contributed to their governments' decision to move toward peace; the economic burden of continuing the war has been enormous for both countries, and the specter of continuously mounting defense outlays was one factor which impelled them to seek a political resolution to the conflict.

Economic processes may yet assume a larger role in the relations between the two countries. In the first place, the facilitation of trade and other forms of economic cooperation has always been regarded by Israel as an essential and integral part of the normalization of relations. Second, and more important, it has been argued that the encouragement of economic cooperation between Egypt and Israel could consolidate what inevitably will be (at least in the beginning) a fragile political construct. There are those who have even ventured to suggest that economic exchanges could spill over into other areas of potential collaboration, thus sustaining and strengthening the process of reconciliation.

Clearly, the opening of commercial relations between Israel and Egypt has encouraged a host of policy questions. Can the prospects for positive gains from economic interaction, considered separately from the gains generated by reduction in the defense burden, offer substantial economic prizes which could serve as an extra inducement to peacemaking? Does economic intercourse per se give rise to conflicts which could harm the fragile structure of peace? Starting from the objective of strengthening peace, which economic transactions should be encouraged and which should be discouraged? These are some of the questions addressed in this article.

It seems that these questions can be usefully tackled by employing economic analysis applied on a more general level and divorced from the specific Egyptian-Israeli context. Accordingly, the concept of vested interest in peace (VIP) is developed to deal with the relationship between welfare gains of different economic actors and the degree of political support for the peace process. Then, the effect of trade between past belligerents on different actors is examined. A scheme facilitating the ranking of bilateral transactions according to their impact on VIP is then outlined, and policy implications discussed. In an appendix, we outline an example which illustrates the usefulness of the concepts developed in this article.

The analysis implies that the scope for mutually beneficial bilateral transactions between neighboring past belligerents is much larger than is commonly assumed on the basis of international trade and economic integration theories. These gains are encouraged since transfer costs (that is, costs of transportation, of international marketing, of communication, of search, and so on) tend to diminish with distance.

Establishment of economic relations between neighboring past belligerents facilitates more than the reallocation of production on the basis of comparative advantage. It facilitates establishment or expansion of industries characterized by economies of scale that could not compete internationally before peace because of the combined inhibiting effects of small domestic markets and transfer costs.

Yet, while peace makes it possible to expand the scope of production and trade, some of these activities raise previously unexplained problems: conflicts over the division of costs and of gains, assumption of new risks, and creation of new vested interests.

Government plays an important role in creating the framework that will maximize the economic benefits from exchange between past belligerents while avoiding asymmetrical dependence. Governments may decide to intervene and encourage VIP-enhancing transactions. Such a policy might be justified, even in economies which advocate the laissez-faire approach as a rule, since there is no necessary correspondence between private gains and VIP. Governments could change the relative attractiveness of transactions by using subsidies, tax relief, or other means.

Our conclusions appear to have more general applicability than simply to the Egyptian-Israeli case. Several economic aspects of the peacemaking process appear to have common characteristics. For example, economic relations between past belligerents inevitably proceed from a zero base; the governments are suspicious of each other, especially in those cases where peace is negotiated between the parties and cannot be imposed unilaterally; each government seeks to avoid excessive dependence on the recent enemy even when the costs are high. The following analysis is therefore couched in terms applicable to two neighboring small countries that initially trade with the rest of the world, but not with each other.

The application, however, can easily be extended. In the first place, the two countries need not be close neighbors. Our findings hold as long as transfer costs between the countries under consideration are relatively low when compared with other countries. In the second place, applicability of the analysis is not limited to past belligerents, that is, to countries which initially do not trade with each other. It is easily extended to pairs of countries (or blocs of countries) which start out by discriminating against each other's traded goods, not only in relation to domestic producers but also vis-à-vis producers from third countries. In this sense, our study intends to contribute to what can be labeled the "economics of reconciliation": the economic consequences of peace are found not to be confined just to the effects of such conditions on the defense sector. A more interesting, though perhaps no less complex, relationship exists between non-defense related economic activity and the attainment of peace.

Vested Interest in Peace

Two countries, A and B, which have been at war with each other for many years, decide to make peace and to establish mutual economic relations. Both governments are, however, concerned about the form and proportions which these relations should be allowed to assume, bearing in mind the fragility of the peace and the likelihood that it is being regarded with suspicion and even hostility by wide sections of the population. It is easy to show that if economic relations between A and B are allowed to develop and activities such as trade in goods, trade in services, investments, and joint ventures take place, economic welfare in both countries can increase. However, international economic transactions, while potentially beneficial to all parties, also tend to spawn conflicts over the distribution of costs and gains between the parties and among different sections of the population within the two countries. These conflicts could easily have internal political repercussions. For the foreseeable future, specific economic transactions are likely to be evaluated by the governments of A and B not only, and not even primarily, on the basis of their economic merits but rather on their expected impact on the acceptance of peace by the public.

The following analysis is based on the assumption that each of the two governments seeks to maximize an objective function, labeled hereafter vested interest in peace (VIP). This function, which can have both positive and negative values, is valued not for itself but rather for its perceived relationship with public support for peace. We assume that economic welfare and political views are related through a simple causal chain. Political support for a policy increases if it can be demonstrated that economic welfare will improve as a result of the policy's implementation. If this view of the formation of political opinions corresponds to reality, then it can be postulated that support for peace will rise if it can be shown to improve economic welfare; it will decline if economic welfare is perceived to be diminished by peace.

The notion that attitudes to political questions, even those involving international relations, are influenced by material considerations is not new. Neither is it confined to Marxist views of politics and economics. For example, Albert O. Hirschman (1945) showed how Nazi Germany deliberately used commercial policy to turn other countries into political clients. This was done by promoting in these countries vested interests in associ-

444 INTERNATIONAL STUDIES QUARTERLY

ation with Germany. German products were offered to importers at discount prices. Alternatively, exporters were offered access on privileged terms to the lucrative but highly protected German market. In time, it became obvious to those engaged in German trade that their continued prosperity depended on their government's support for German politics. Powerful pro-German lobbies were thus created in many of Germany's trading partners, especially in the Balkan states (Hirschman, 1945). Generalizing from this experience Hirschman (1945: 29) says:

> If exports are concentrated in some region or industry, not only will the difficulty of adjustment in the case of loss of these exports weigh upon the decision of the governments, but these regions or industries will exert a powerful influence in favor of a "friendly" attitude toward the state to the imports of which they owe their existence. . . .
>
> In the social pattern of each country there exist certain powerful groups the support of which is particularly valuable to a *foreign* country in its power policy; the foreign country will therefore try to establish commercial relations especially with these groups, in order that their voices will be raised in its favor.

Our definition of VIP and the description of the factors determining it may appear as overly pessimistic. This approach apparently suggests that people's views are formed in response to their immediate and short-term material interest; even their economic calculations are extremely myopic, because they ignore the benefits from the reduction in the defense burden which peace must ultimately make possible.

This is not necessarily the case. Public attitude to peace is obviously influenced by many factors, political, psychological, ideological, as well as economic.[1] Peace may be fragile, not because it conflicts with narrow economic interests within the countries concerned, but rather because of the genuine political differences and the difficulties in finding compromises among conflicting claims. In these circumstances, it makes sense to

---

1. See Aron (1966: ch. 3) for a detailed discussion of the relationship between economic factors and attitude towards war in Europe.

promote activities, economic and noneconomic, that will increase the support for the peace process by demonstrating its benefits. It makes equally good sense to refrain from promotion of activities that make peace seem less economically palatable.

International trade theory shows that, under most circumstances, international transactions voluntarily assumed are Pareto-optimal. Overall and even individual welfare can be increased, since the extra real income made available by the exchange could be distributed among the citizens of the country in question (Arrow, 1951: chapter 4). There is, however, no automatic mechanism assuring such redistribution, and thus it may well be that while some individuals gain, others lose. The effect of international transactions on VIP is, therefore, indeterminate unless steps are taken either to compensate those whose welfare is adversely affected or to impose restrictions on international transactions. In the second case, only transactions the overall economic benefits of which are clearly discernible and which cause no economic injury to politically articulate sections of the population will be allowed.

The first alternative, that of compensating those injured by international transactions, appears to be ruled out. Its realization is handicapped by endless conceptual and administrative difficulties due to the problems involved in identifying and measuring injuries caused by international transactions. Moreover, it is extremely difficult to devise equitable and administratively feasible methods of compensation. Finally, even if these difficulties could be overcome, there is no assurance that the measures would indeed be adopted. The second option (allowing only those transactions which cause no injury to politically powerful groups) may consequently be preferred in practice.

To clarify the above statement, it is useful to distinguish between two interest groups affected by international economic transactions: producers and consumers.

Producers are those involved in the production of goods and services whose output is directly affected by the economic transactions under consideration—entrepreneurs, shareholders, employees, suppliers, subcontractors, and so on. Consumers are those who purchase the goods and services referred to above.

A producer's welfare rises when rents and profits go up, that is, when revenues increase more than costs.[2] Consumer welfare in the present context is affected simply by price changes. When prices rise, consumer welfare declines; when prices decline, consumer welfare rises.

The interests of these two groups do not necessarily coincide when considering the welfare effects of peace. For example, when the price of a given good goes up, its producers benefit and consumers lose. Decline in price may result in the curtailment of production and output: consumers benefit, producers lose, and employment in the industry manufacturing the good may be curtailed.

If there were no possible divergence of interest between the groups discussed above, there would be no need to bother about the determination of VIP. VIP in this case would coincide or at least have a one to one relationship with conventional economic welfare. Transactions which can be shown to improve welfare increase VIP and vice versa.[3]

How can conflict between the groups be resolved? In the present context, the answer is obvious: the political process. Before proceeding with the discussion it is necessary, therefore, to rank the interest groups on the basis of their presumed political power. We assume that producer interests receive a higher priority by governments than consumer interests, and that governments are particularly sensitive to employment. Specifically, we assume that economic transactions between A and B which can be shown to result in closure of plants or curtailment of employment will simply not be tolerated.

The notion that producers' interests dominate the economy was argued as early as 1935, when E. E. Schattschneider stated that "the consumers are at least as numerous as any other group

2. Producers may include several subgroups who must share the welfare gains accruing to the entire group. We assume here that when the group benefits from net gains it shares them in a way which raises the welfare of each subgroup.

3. Alternatively, if it could be assumed that the "compensation principle" would in fact be applied and those injured by competition from abroad would be compensated, VIP would be equated with economic welfare also in this case. However, if compensation cannot be guaranteed, there is no necessary correspondence between VIP and conventional welfare gains.

in the society, but they have no organization to countervail the power of organized or monopolistic producers" (cited in Olson, 1965: 128).

A similar argument was put forward by Key (1958: 56): "The lobbyists for electrical utilities, for example, are eternally on the job; the lobbyists for the consumers of this monopolistic service are ordinarily conspicuous by their absence."

Olson (1965) took up this idea and developed it further, arguing that the organization of producers and the relatively small number of firms comprising each industry make the producers what he calls (1965: 128) an "intermediate" if not a privileged group "with the political power that naturally and necessarily flows to those that control the business and property of the country." Consumers, on the other hand, form a large, unorganized group, the members of which "are organized only in special circumstances, but business interests are organized as a general rule."

Thomas Lachs (1979) refers to governments embedding this "producer's dominance" consideration in their policies.[4] "It is a fact that in capitalist societies . . . governments have always developed their economic policy in close coordination with business interests. This is presumably a necessity and not even socialist governments have been able to act differently."[5]

Initiating Trade Between Past
Belligerents—A Classification Scheme

Having outlined the relationship between vested interest in peace (VIP) and the factors which determine it, we turn to the examination of specific international economic transactions, that is, international trade, with a view to evaluating their effect on VIP. The framework and the terminology used in analyzing the effects of trade are both adapted from economic integration

---

4. Such considerations have been used in studies of trade policy such as Blackhurst et al. (1977: 32-3), and in many regulation studies such as Wilson (1974) and Doron (1979).

5. Thomas Lachs's comment on Blyth (1978) is cited in OECD (1979: 97).

theory, which deals with the effects of reducing or abolishing tariffs on welfare (Viner, 1950; Balassa, 1962).

Integration theory distinguishes between two effects of tariff reduction: trade creation and trade diversion. Trade creation takes place when, following the abolition of tariffs between A and B (after the establishment of a free trade area between them), A, instead of producing high cost goods in which it has no comparative advantage, imports them from B. Trade diversion takes place when A stops importing goods from C, a low-cost producer whose imports are subjected to tariffs, and shifts to importing from B, a high-cost producer, and member of the free trade area. Trade creation is welfare-enhancing while trade diversion has the effect of reducing welfare. Since the establishment of a free trade area results in both effects, it is impossible to state on a priori grounds whether the overall effect is to increase or decrease welfare.[6]

The situation considered here differs from that of received integration theory in two important respects: integration theory deals with the case where two countries A and B grant each other concessions which are *denied* to the rest of the world. The present discussion focuses on the case where A and B agree to *reduce discrimination* between them and to treat each other in the same way that they treat the rest of the world.[7] Preferences encourage trade creation and trade diversion, as we have seen; hence welfare may either increase or decrease. Ending discrimination cannot decrease welfare, since it diversifies the sources of supply and increases the choice available to consumers.

Moreover, there is a basic difference in the treatment of welfare effects in the two cases. Integration theory focuses rightly and properly on *consumption*. A country's welfare is increased if it can consume more as a result of engaging in certain transactions. In the present case, alternative outcomes are not evaluated on the basis of their effect on overall welfare. Potential benefits and

6. For a detailed survey of the literature dealing with the conditions under which integration leads to welfare gains or losses, see Lipsey (1960) and Krauss (1972). For a discussion of the modern versions of the theory, see Berglas (1979).

7. They may be viewed as reducing infinite tariffs imposed on trade between them to the level applied to the rest of the world. However, there may be limits to the elimination of discrimination between past belligerents seeking to promote VIP.

costs are valued on the basis of their impact on different groups of actors whose welfare is weighed according to their political clout.

These considerations lead to concepts similar to those used in integration theory in terms which make them more useful for the analysis of the relationship between trade and VIP. Before defining these concepts a brief outline of the analytical framework is presented.

The framework of the following analysis is that of partial equilibrium, which is commonly used by integration theorists and is particularly useful for identification of the immediate impact of trade flows on the welfare of different economic actors. In the present case, the partial equilibrium framework is particularly appropriate because the analysis focuses on specific transactions which are unlikely to affect the entire economy. Moreover, even the sum total of the bilateral transactions between past belligerents is unlikely to account for a substantial share of their total international transactions, at least in the short run. Macro-economic effects, for which a general equilibrium framework is more suitable, can therefore be ignored.

Reference is made as before to two countries A and B (the past belligerents) and to a third country R (the rest of the world). The point of view is that of country A. The government of A considers the likely effect of exporting a specific good on VIP in *both* countries. A and B are small countries; both are price takers. They trade with the rest of the world. International supply and demand schedules are infinitely elastic. Cost functions of two types are considered: increasing costs and decreasing costs.

In the first case, the product and factor markets are assumed to be perfectly competitive. Aggregate cost functions are obtained by horizontally adding up the quantities produced by the individual enterprises at different prices.[8] In the second case, presence of economies of scale is assumed to imply that at most, one efficient plant is needed to supply the domestic market in A and B.[9]

8. Actually, aggregate cost functions are likely to rise at a higher rate than individual cost functions, if we take into account the likelihood that as all individual enterprises in a given industry seek to expand output they will run into input-price increases not encountered by an individual enterprise which decides to expand.

9. Recall that A and B are small countries.

The increasing marginal cost case is more suitable for the analysis of short term effects, that is, the time span during which output capacity cannot be adjusted to meet changes in external conditions. In the long run, capacity can be expanded. Long-term average costs are likely to be horizontal in the absence of scale economies and U-shaped if economies of scale exist.[10] It is therefore possible to treat the increasing and decreasing cost cases as reflecting the short and the long terms, respectively.

Before finishing with the preliminaries, it is necessary to define transfer costs. This term refers to the cost incurred in moving goods between the producers located in one country and their foreign customers. Transfer costs include transportation costs and the excess of export over domestic marketing costs.[11] Tariffs are not considered part of transfer costs, though their inclusion would not affect the outcome provided A is granted Most Favored Nation status in B. In trade and integration theory, transfer costs are usually assumed to be equal to zero. In the present case, transfer costs are crucially important.

Specifically, we assume transfer costs between A and R and B and R to be positive and equal, and transfer costs between A and B to be negligible. Transfer costs between A and B are small partly because of physical distance, which affects the costs of transportation. There are, however, additional sources of cost savings. Many of the fixed and variable costs involved in international marketing can be substantially reduced. It may be possible, for example, to save on storage facilities and on inventories. Double handling in shipping may be eliminated. In addition, customers may be served directly by the manufacturer rather than by separate service organizations.

Physical proximity between trading partners is also likely to help reduce another important trade barrier: cultural distance. Cultural, like physical, distance initiates costs due to differences in language, in customs, in the ways of "doing business" and, of course, in consumer tastes. The costs involved in overcoming

10. The shapes, however, could be modified by the macro-effects mentioned in note 8.

11. For a discussion of the difference between domestic and export marketing costs, see Hirsch (1976).

cultural distance may constitute formidable trade barriers which could in many cases overwhelm the cost advantage due to the traditional "comparative advantage."[12] Between neighboring countries, these costs presumably decline over time, as experience accumulates and as the population, especially that section which lives along the borders of the two countries, acquires better knowledge of the conditions prevailing on the other side.[13]

There remain, of course, the man-made trade barriers represented by import duties and a host of trade restrictions and administrative regulations which hamper the flow of goods and services. These may or may not be reduced as part of the peace process. It is, however, possible to conclude that, other things being equal and unless A discriminates deliberately against B relative to R, physical proximity is likely to reduce trade barriers between A and B. The ending of belligerency between A and B consequently affects their bilateral trade potential much more if they are neighbors than if they have no common borders.

Next, let us consider the different effects of opening up trade between neighboring past belligerents. The following effects are distinguished: export diversion, import creation, export expansion, export creation, and output creation. The terms have definite hierarchic connotations and refer to the rank ordering of the VIP function.

EXPORT DIVERSION

Export diversion[14] is illustrated in Figures 1 and 2. In Figure 1, which shows the rising cost case, the domestic market is shown

12. Indeed, writers such as Burenstam-Linder (1961) advanced the proposition that trade between countries declines as the cultural distance (measured by difference in per capita income) increases. This proposition conflicts with expectations derived from the Heckscher-Ohlin model. For an attempt to reconcile the two models, see Arad and Hirsch (1979).

13. The proposition mentioned is supported by the mounting evidence of large-scale smuggling taking place between Israel and Egypt following the signing of the Peace Treaty.

14. Tovias (1977) uses a similar term—export trade diversion—to describe the effect of preference agreements on the direction of exports. The policy instrument in Tovias' model is tariff reduction. In this case it is removal of discrimination. The welfare effects are consequently different.

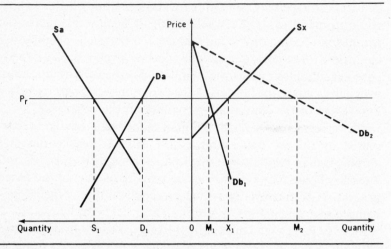

Figure 1: Export Diversion—Increasing Costs

separately from the world market. Domestic demand and supply schedules in A are shown on the left hand side, where the quantity axis increases in value from right to left. S_a is A's supply curve (obtained by horizontally adding up the marginal cost curves of all the producers in A who are competing against each other). S_x is A's excess supply curve: it represents A's offer of exports and is obtained by deducting for different prices the quantity demanded domestically from the quantity supplied. P_r is the demand of the rest of the world, which is infinitely elastic.

Export diversion takes place when transfer costs are equal to zero. As long as A is barred from supplying B, it produces S_1 and exports X_1 to R, selling the difference $D_1 (D_1 = S_1 - X_1)$ in the domestic market.

B's excess demand curve D_b is shown to the right of the price axis.[15] At world market price P_r, B imports M_1 from R. When imports from A are admitted into B, imports from A could vary from zero to M_1. A's exporters, however, are likely to have an edge over R because of the physical proximity between the countries. If this edge allows them to shed their price even by

15. The excess demand curve is derived (similarly to excess supply) by deducting for each price the quantity supplied domestically from the quantity demanded.

an infinitesimal amount, A's exporters could capture a high share of B's import market. In that case, A's exports to R decline. At the margin, A's exports to R decline from X_l to $X_l - M_l$. The amount $X_l - M_l$ represents export diversion from R to B. If D_b intersects S_x to the right of X_l and A sells all its exports to B, the price remains P_r, B imports X_l from A and $M_2 - X_l$ from R. In that case export diversion is equal to A's total exports.

The decreasing cost case is shown in Figure 2. World price P_r is above the point where long run average costs, LAC_a, reaches the minimum. A produces S_a (which is not smaller than Q_{min}—the minimum efficient plant size), selling D_l ($D_l < S_a$) in the domestic market and $S_a - D_l$ in R. S_a is the point of intersection between the original marginal cost-curve (not shown) and the world price. When trade between A and B is permitted, B imports M_l from A. $M_l < \max[S_a - D_l, M_o]$, where M_o is B's pre-peace imports from R. M_l is diverted from other markets provided A, due to its proximity to B, has some infinitesimal cost advantage over R. Note that this outcome depends on LAC_a's minimum point being *below* P_r. If P_r is below the minimum point of LAC_a, A will neither export nor produce and A's (as well as B's) consumption will be imported from R.

IMPORT EXPANSION AND EXPORT EXPANSION

For import expansion to take place, transfer costs must be positive. To simplify the analysis we assume that fixed transfer costs are equal to zero and that variable unit transfer costs are constant. The following notation is used:

P_a domestic market price in A;

t   unit transfer costs;

$P_r - t$ export receipts per unit exported to R;

$P_r + t$ cost per unit imported from R.

Consider first the case where marginal costs rise. The effects of introducing trade between A and B in this case are shown in Figure 3. Transfer costs, though positive, do not prevent A from

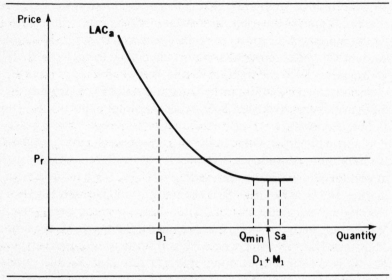

Figure 2: Export Diversion—Decreasing Costs

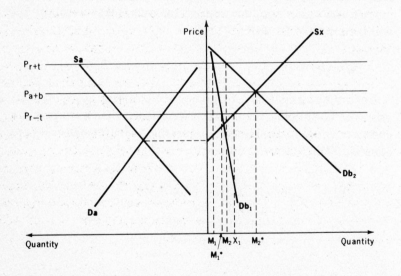

Figure 3: Import Expansion and Export Expansion—Increasing Costs

exporting to R. A's exporters receive $P_r - t$, which equals the domestic price in A (P_a). Quantity exported is X_1. If A's exports are admitted into B, whose excess demand is D_{b1}, exports will be diverted from R to B. Total exports remain at X_1 though the share of R in A's exports declines from 100% to $(X_1 - M_1^*) \div X_1$. The situation from B's point of view has, however, changed. Instead of importing M_1 from R at the price of $P_r + t$, B now imports M_1^* at a lower price, $P_r - t$. The case where export prices and receipts remain unchanged in A, despite the increase in B's imports, is labeled import expansion.

The situation is different if B's excess demand is large enough to divert all of A's exports away from R. This is the case when B's demand schedule is D_{b2}. Here, B's imports increase from M_2 to M_2^* and A's exports increase from X_1 to M_2^*. Prices received by A's exporters rise from $P_r - t$ to P_{a+b} and prices paid by B's consumers decline from $P_r - t$ to P_{a+b}. To distinguish this last case from the previous one where A's export prices and quantities remained unchanged, we label it export expansion.

The decreasing cost version of import expansion is shown in Figure 4. Before peace, A produces S_a, sells D_a in the domestic market and exports $S_a - D_a$. B imports M_1 at the price $P_r + t$. When imports from A are admitted, B imports M_1^* ($M_1^* > M_1$), paying $P_r - t$ ($P_r - t < P_r + t$).[16]

EXPORT CREATION AND OUTPUT CREATION

Export creation is the decreasing cost equivalent of export expansion. The reason for the difference in the labels is demonstrated in Figure 5. Here, the minimum cost point of LAC_a is *above* $P_r - t$. A can therefore under no circumstances export to R. Whether production takes place depends on whether domestic demand intersects with LAC_a to the left or to the right

16. A similar case is discussed in Corden (1972), where the gains from expanding output of products enjoying economies of scale are labeled "cost reduction effects." In Corden's example (1972: 468), gains from cost reduction may be counterbalanced by losses due to trade suppression effects "which take place when a dear source replaces a cheap one with the formation of a customs union."

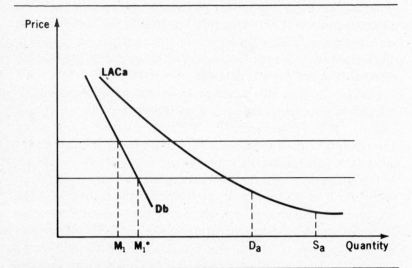

Figure 4: Import Expansion—Decreasing Costs

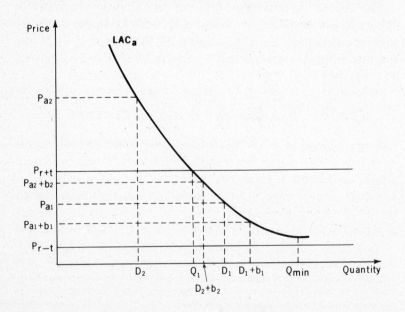

Figure 5: Export and Output Creation

of Q_1. If the curves intersect to the right of Q_1 at D_1, A's consumers can be charged a price bounded by P_{a1} and $P_r + t$ ($P_{a1} <$ $P_r + t$, where $P_r + t$ is the import price).[17] A's costs will move along the declining LAC_a curve. The cost of producing for both markets at D_{1+b1} will be P_{a1+b1}. The opening of B's market transforms A from a domestic into an international producer. Thus, this case is labeled export creation.

Finally, consider output creation, also illustrated in Figure 5. Here, domestic demand (not shown) and LAC_a intersect to the left of Q_1 at D_s ($P_{a2} > P_r + t$). Imports are less costly than domestic production. If demand of A plus B intersects LAC_a to the right of Q_1 at D_{2+b2}, then the opening of B's market is a condition not only for exports but also for production in A. Hence the label output creation.

The Effect of Trade on Welfare and on VIP

The different trade effects are summarized in Table 1, which ranks the effects according to their impact on welfare in the two countries and on VIP. The ranking scheme proposed here is based on immediate or first order effects only. When considering the effect of a transaction, we consider only the impact on employment, profits, price of output, and so on, of the enterprises immediately affected. Secondary effects, that is, effects on suppliers and on other sectors, are ignored.

Export diversion has no welfare effects. Consumers do not pay lower prices and producers do not receive higher revenues. Consequently, the VIP ranking of export diversion is necessarily low. Note that this conclusion holds regardless of the volume of trade diverted from R to B. Even if B's entire imports are switched to A and even if B becomes A's major customer when trade between the two countries is allowed, there are only infinitesimal gains in consumers' and producers' welfare in the two countries. This conclusion holds regardless of whether marginal costs are rising or declining: Though A and B refrained from

17. The actual price in A will depend on the extent to which A's producer-monopolist is able to exercise pricing power.

TABLE 1
Different Trade Effects and Their Impact on VIP

| | Costs | | Welfare Effects | | | | |
	Production	Transfer	Consumer A	B	Producers A	Others in A	VIP Rank
Export Diversion	rise	0	0	0	0	no	1
	decline	0	0	0	0	no	
Import Expansion	rise	+	0	+	0	no	2
	decline	+	0	+	0	no	
Export Expansion	rise	+	−	+	+	export, output rise	3
Export Creation	decline	+	+	+	+	export, output rise	4
Output Creation	decline	+	+	+	+	new investment	5

NOTE: With the exception of export diversion, output, and employment increase in B's industries manufacturing complementary goods and services, and decrease in those manufacturing competing goods and services. The ranking assumes that government policy in B prevents import competition from affecting employment adversely.

trading with each other before the conclusion of peace, their economies were in fact interconnected via their trade with R. When trade is opened up, there are no additional welfare gains to be made.

When import expansion takes place, consumers in B benefit, because they obtain more imports at lower prices than before. The welfare of consumers and producers in A remains unaffected, since total value of exports from A remains fixed regardless of whether marginal costs of production rise or decline. Since nobody's welfare is adversely affected by import expansion, it gets a higher VIP rank than export diversion.

Export expansion affects welfare of consumers in A and B and of producers in A. While consumer welfare in B increases ($P_{a+b} < P_r + t$), that of A's consumers declines ($P_{a+b} > P_r - t$). A's producers receive a higher price for a larger output: their welfare rises, of course. Bearing in mind the earlier discussion concerning the relative political power of consumers and producers and recalling that B's consumers benefit, we conclude that export expansion has an overall positive effect on VIP (in both countries) even though one sector of A's population is hurt. Export expansion ranks third on the VIP ranking scale.[18]

Export creation and output creation have positive welfare effects on all the relevant actors. Costs decline as a result of moving along the declining cost curve. Producers in A need not pass on all their costs savings to the consumers; but even if they charge prices which equate marginal revenues with marginal costs in both countries, they have to reduce prices to sell their higher output. Consumers in A and B will consequently enjoy net gains.[19]

Output creation offers additional benefits. In the first place, producers in A and consumers in A and B benefit from expansion of output and reduction in costs as in the case of export creation.

18. Obviously if consumers are politically more powerful, export expansion might be ranked lower than export diversion, which offers no welfare gains.

19. Analytically, output creation is similar to Corden's trade suppression. The difference between the overall welfare effects of output creation (which is positive) and trade suppression (which is negative) is due to the presence of transfer costs, which are nonexistent in Corden's model.

Employment is increased, as in the case of export expansion. The effect of output creation on VIP is expected to be greater than that of export creation. While both have a positive impact on the economic welfare of *all* the relevant actors in both countries, output creation is the only case where peace makes it possible to establish an industry which is unable to compete internationally unless trade between A and B takes place. No other situation discussed thus far has such a clear-cut and easily identifiable positive impact.

Thus, without having to measure and compare the welfare of the different actors, and while making only a single (and we hope plausible) assumption about the relative political power of the relevant actors, it is possible to rank the different trade effects according to their expected impact on VIP.[20]

Policy Implications

While the grouping of the transactions according to their trade effects and to their impact on VIP has implications for policy-making, no specific policy has been indicated. Moreover, adoption of the ranking scheme outlined in Table 1 is consistent with different policies ranging from complete laissez-faire through detailed intervention in individual transactions. None of the transactions is welfare-reducing in either A or B when welfare is considered in the conventional sense of the word. Export diversion has neither positive nor negative conventional welfare effects. With the exception of import expansion, which increases welfare only in B, all the remaining transactions enhance welfare in both countries, since these transactions follow the *elimination* of discriminating restrictions and not the institution of discrimination (as is the case when two countries establish a free trade area or grant each other preferences).

20. Note, however, that the ranks might be changed in specific cases when information about the second order effects is available. Note also that the scheme ignores effects on producers in B, which may be positive if the latter produce complementary goods or negative if they manufacture competing products.

Thus, if A's government believes in laissez-faire, it might decide to refrain from interfering in or influencing the decisions of domestic firms concerning exports to B. In this case, there is no need to distinguish among the different kinds of transactions discussed above. Firms in A will presumably make their own calculations and will decide whether and how much to export to B on the basis of expected prices, sales, costs, risk, and so on. Even a laissez-faire oriented government in B will, on the other hand, restrict those imports which reduce producer welfare because of their adverse effects on VIP.[21] It will, however, be indifferent to those imports which do not compete with local production, regardless of the category to which they belong.

Governments may decide to adopt a more interventionist policy and to discriminate among the different groups of transactions. Such discrimination could be justified on the grounds of (1) contribution to VIP, (2) risk assumed by the enterprises engaged in trade, and (3) effect on interdependence.

The contribution to VIP of the different transactions was discussed above and need not be repeated here. Since there is no necessary correspondence between private gain and VIP, the government could help to change the relative attractiveness of the transactions, offering higher incentives for export creation than for export expansion, for example. If this policy is adopted, the government could be guided by ranking schemes of the kind outlined in Table 1.[22]

Similar considerations apply to the treatment of risk. Obviously, economic transactions with a past belligerent will be viewed as more risky by individual enterprises than trading with established customers. These risks emanate from the lack of knowledge and information about the market. In time, these particular risks are likely to disappear, but when economic transactions are in their initial stages, they may constitute a

21. Actually, competing imports, which are assumed here to have negative effects on VIP, are precisely those transactions which integration theory labels "trade creating" and which are regarded as welfare enhancing. This conflict between the policy implications of integration theory and the present approach is explained by our assumptions about the political predominance of producer over consumer interests in government decision-making.

22. Note, however, the cautionary remark in footnote 20.

barrier. The ranking scheme of Table 1 offers a guide to the relative riskiness of these transactions. Export diversion and import expansion, for example, are not very risky; when transfer costs are negligible, A firms are indifferent as to whether they export to B or to R. Similarly, risks are small even if transfer costs are positive when the freight on board price charged in the different markets is the same and shipments can be shifted between B and R in both directions without incurring losses. Export expansion involves higher risks since it is likely to require additional resources, including labor and possibly investment in production facilities. Export creation is still more risky. It requires, in addition to the above, commitment of resources to the development of the export marketing, a function with which the enterprises in question are unfamiliar by definition.[23] Output creation is more risky than export creation, since it pertains to the manufacture of new products which must be marketed in both A and B if they are to be internationally competitive.

Next, we consider the effect of the different transactions on dependence. In the context of peacemaking, dependence (and its obverse, interdependence) was defined elsewhere as the extent to which A and B enter into economic relations which prove costly to break. Dependence is thus related to the cost of dissociation (Waltz, 1970; Hirschman, 1945).

Clearly, the transactions discussed above contribute differently to dependence of A on B and vice versa. Their ranking according to their impact on dependence is in fact the same as that of risk. Transactions which were here identified as riskier from A's point of view are also costlier to annul. Thus, establishment in A of an industry which depends for its survival on exports to B is riskier than shifting existing exports from R to B. The higher risks are caused by the lack of alternative markets in the first case and by the potential bankruptcy faced by A's enterprises if exports to B are discontinued.[24] Risks are higher still when A depends on B not only for markets but also for inputs, as in the case of joint ventures.[25]

23. Note that risk and VIP considerations do not produce identical ranks. Export expansion has a higher risk than VIP rank.

24. B also assumes risks in relying on supplies from A. The risks and the costs involved are not the same in both countries. In most cases, the risk assumed by B is lower.

25. These risks are, however, neutralized to a certain extent due to the dependence of B on A for markets for the input it supplies to the "joint venture."

The policy instruments likely to be used by the government to promote VIP, to handle risk, and to uphold interdependence are quite different. In the first case, fiscal measures—including subsidies, grants and tax relief—may be most appropriate. In the second case, insurance schemes may be preferred. In the third case, administrative intervention may be deemed necessary. In all cases, however, the same information is required by the decision maker. The concepts developed in this article should help in identifying the type of information needed and in evaluating its usefulness in the context of initiating trade between past belligerents. A possibly significant example of potential trade between Egypt and Israel is considered in the Appendix.

The effect of imports from A on production in B has been incompletely treated thus far. The negative effect of import competition on VIP was assumed away by stating that transactions which will hurt the politically powerful producers will be disallowed. At first glance it appears that if A and B grant each other Most Favored Nation status, the problem is resolved. Governments can be assumed to establish import regulations which provide import-competing sectors with a degree of protection consistent with the "national interest." Note, however, that B's pre-peace commercial policy is presumably designed to give domestic producers an acceptable degree of protection vis-à-vis R's producers. Since the latter are handicapped by transfer costs, the degree of protection given to B's marginal producer against imports from R may be insufficient to protect them against imports from A. Consequently, if B's producers are to enjoy the same degree of protection against A's as against R's producers, higher tariffs may have to be charged on imports from A. If A's government wishes to promote VIP in B, it will accept some degree of discrimination against its exporters, even though this entails departure from the Most Favored Nation principle.[26]

26. Alternatively, MFN could be reformulated on a CIF basis, thus allowing A's and R's exporters to compete on an equal footing in B. The discriminatory advantage which transfer costs confer on some traders is discussed in a recent article by A.J. Yeats (1980), who argues that CIF based tariff valuation often discriminates against the developing countries. He suggests that some of this discrimination can be removed by changing the valuation basis from CIF to FOB. This suggestion is in line with the approach suggested here.

Conclusion

Our analysis has shown that economic effects of transition from war to peace are not confined to the gains that can be derived from reducing the defense burden on the one hand, and to the costs involved in scaling down the defense industries and reallocation of employment and investment in the economy on the other. Substantial gains may be derived from bilateral transactions between the past belligerents and from reorientation of their economies towards each other.

The potential for economic cooperation between past belligerents who happen to be neighbors is likely to be greater and more varied than it would be between any other pair of countries. The potential gains from "normal" trade between them is limited, especially if the countries in question are small and if they have been extensively engaged in international trade prior to concluding peace between them. In that case, even if substantial trade is diverted from third countries, it is unlikely to affect relative costs by more than a fraction. The real prizes can be found elsewhere; not in the two countries' existing trade, but rather among those goods and services which were previously considered non-tradeable, that is, those goods and services which were either not produced at all, or, if produced, were not exported, due to the high cost of international transfer. It is the *expansion of the tradeables sector* which may well be the source of most substantial gains from economic intercourse between past belligerents.

APPENDIX

A Possible Example

The usefulness of the concepts introduced in the previous sections is illustrated by a concrete example involving the Egyptian-Israeli peace process.[27] The example considered here pertains to the cement industry, whose economic and technolog-

27. Based on a preliminary study by S. Bahiri of the Israel Institute of Business Research at Tel Aviv University.

ical characteristics qualify it as a possible candidate for economic cooperation between the two countries.

Cement is a bulky product whose value relative to its weight is low. It is consequently not usually transported over long distances. The production process is subject to significant economies of scale, and the minimum size of an efficient plant is large. When a new plant is built, the addition to a small country's production capacity can be quite substantial. Thus, temporary excess capacity is often found in a country or region where a new plant was recently completed. Since the production process is highly capital-intensive and since marginal costs are low, it pays to produce at full capacity and to export the surplus, as long as prices exceed marginal costs. This alternative is preferred to production at less than full capacity, which raises unit costs substantially. Exports are only temporary as a rule, since capacity is designed to take care of "normal" domestic demand. As domestic demand expands, exports are first reduced and finally discontinued. If and when domestic demand expands further, temporary imports are required to take care of it, since expansion implies substantial increase in capacity that cannot be effected at short notice.

The timing of new investments and their volume is rather tricky, particularly in small countries, because of the bulkiness of the investment. Thus, small countries are likely to depend more on foreign trade in cement than large countries. Dependence on foreign trade in cement is undesirable because of the high cost of transportation coupled with substantial uncertainties associated with supplies, markets, and prices.

Cooperation between Egypt and Israel in the cement industry could be beneficial to both countries in several respects. If trade barriers to cement are eliminated, the two countries can form a single market, thus benefiting from economies of scale and being less dependent on erratic markets and suppliers.

As of the end of 1980, both Egypt (with six plants) and Israel (with three) have been rather short of cement and both countries have been planning to increase their production capacity over the coming years. The establishment of economic relations between the two countries poses some interesting questions regarding the location of Israel's fourth plant. The plant could conceivably be located in Egypt rather than Israel, since Egypt enjoys a considerable cost advantage in energy, which is intensively used in the manufacture of cement. Cost savings in energy could compensate for the higher transportation costs incurred in shipping cement over longer distances. Tentative calculations indicate that a plant located in Egypt could compete with an Israeli plant in the Israeli market if the former could obtain gas at a price representing a 30%-35% discount over the cost of energy obtained from coal imported by Israel. A transaction of this kind is conceivably profitable for Egypt, considering the alternative uses for its gas.

Assuming that this is indeed the case, let us see how some of the concepts developed earlier can be used to gain additional insights into the possible effects of the transactions on the two countries.

The cement project described above obviously belongs to the *export creation* category. Peaceful relations with Israel make it possible to establish in Egypt a potentially welfare-enhancing new export industry which will earn urgently needed foreign exchange. If prices are competitive, consumer welfare in Israel, too, will be raised.[28] Other factors must, however, be examined as well. Consider the nature and extent of mutual dependence which the project generates. Egyptian plants each employing approximately over one hundred people become dependent on a single foreign market. Bearing in mind the high transportation costs, it is unlikely that alternative export markets will be profitable. As for the Israelis, they depend on a single foreign supplier for about one-quarter of their cement, which is an important material in the construction industry. If supplies are discontinued, alternative sources are bound to be more expensive. Both sides should consider additional risks: If Egyptian domestic demand rises, will prices be raised or supplies diverted? If demand in Israel slackens, will the Israelis reduce domestic purchases, or will they rather reduce their imports?

Questions such as these inevitably surface whenever a bulky investment project is being considered. In the present context, however, it is not only the economic welfare of those affected by

---

28. Recall that the alternative is to build a more expensive plant in Israel.

the decision which is at stake; the peace process, too, may be affected, since it is the recent enemy which appears responsible for both the gains from cooperation and the losses caused by disruption. Clearly, no government can be indifferent to either possibility. It is for this reason that governments play an important role in establishing the rules which govern the volume and form of bilateral transactions between recent belligerents.

Date of receipt of final manuscript: May 18, 1981

REFERENCES

ARAD, R. and S. HIRSCH (1979) "Determinants of trade flows and choice of trade partners: reconciling the Heckscher-Ohlin, Burenstam-Linder, and the technology gap models of international trade." Working Paper 619/79, The Israel Institute of Business Research, Tel Aviv University. (mimeo)

ARON, R. (1966) The Century of Total War. Boston: Beacon.

ARROW, K. J. (1951) Social Choice and Individual Values. New Haven: Yale Univ. Press.

BALASSA, B. (1962) Theory of Economic Integration. Homewood, IL: Irwin.

BERGLAS, E. (1979) "Preferential trading theory: the n commodity case." J. of Pol. Economy 87, 2 (April): 315-331.

BLACKHURST, R., N. MARIAN, and J. TUMLIR (1977) Trade Liberalization Protectionism and Interdependence. Geneva: GATT.

BLYTH, C. A. (1978) "The interaction between collective bargaining and government policies in selected member countries." Presented at the conference Collective Bargaining and Government Policies, Washington, DC, July 10-13.

BURENSTAM-LINDER, S. (1961) An Essay on Trade and Transformation. New York: John Wiley.

CORDEN, W. M. (1972) "Economies of scale and customs union theory." J. of Pol. Economy 80: 465-475.

DORON, G. (1979) The Smoking Paradox: Public Regulation in the Cigarette Industry. Cambridge, MA: Abt.

HIRSCH, S. (1976) "An international trade and investment theory of the firm." Oxford Econ. Papers 28, 2: 258-270.

HIRSCHMAN, A. O. (1945) National Power and the Structure of Foreign Trade. Berkeley: Univ. of California Press.

KEY, V. O., Jr. (1958) Politics, Parties and Pressure Groups, 4th ed. New York: Crowell.

KRAUSS, M. B. (1972) "Recent developments in customs union theory: an interpretative survey." J. of Econ. Literature 10 (June).

LIPSEY, R. G. (1960) "The theory of customs unions: a general survey." Econ. J. 70 (September): 496-513.

Organization for Economic Cooperation and Development (1979) Collective Bargaining and Government Policies, 1978. Paris: Author.

OLSON, M., Jr. (1965) The Logic of Collective Action: Public Goods and the Theory of Groups. Cambridge, MA: Harvard Univ. Press.

SCHATTSCHNEIDER, E. E. (1935) Politics, Pressures and the Tariff. Englewood Cliffs, NJ: Prentice-Hall.

TOVIAS, A. (1977) Tariff Preferences in Mediterranean Diplomacy. London: Macmillan.

VINER, J. (1950) The Customs Union Issue. New York: Carnegie Endowment for International Peace.

WALTZ, K. (1970) "The myth of national interdependence," in C. P. Kindleberger (ed.) The Multinational Corporation. Cambridge, MA: MIT Press.

WILSON, J. A. (1974) "The politics of regulation," in J. W. McKie (ed.) Social Responsibility and the Business Predicament. Washington, DC: Brookings Institution.

YEATS, A. J. (1980) "Tariff valuation, transport costs, and the establishment of trade preferences among developing countries." World Development 8, 2: 129-136.

The Important Commonwealth

A Behavioral Indicator

JAMES H. POLHEMUS

School of Social Sciences
Deakin University (Victoria, Australia)

Level of attendance at 22 Commonwealth Prime Ministers/Heads of Government meetings (1944-1979) is used as an indicator to test several propositions concerning the importance of the Commonwealth to its member states. According to the indicator: (1) the Commonwealth has diminished in importance although not to the extent anticipated; (2) it is of more importance to old than to new members; (3) nevertheless, the Commonwealth is of more importance to new Commonwealth states than are the Organization of African Unity or the Nonaligned Movement; (4) the Commonwealth is less important to republics than to dominions or other monarchies; and (5) first generation leaders of new Commonwealth states attach more importance to the Commonwealth than do second generation leaders, especially when the latter have come to power by extraconstitutional means. It is proposed that a watch over levels of attendance is a useful means of monitoring the health of international summit conferencing systems like the Commonwealth.

Commentators on the Commonwealth habitually exhibit uncertainty about the health and survival of their subject. If few are prepared to prescribe its demise, most seem to seek a position from which they need not be excessively embarrassed in the event that the Commonwealth expires or is transformed beyond recognition.[1] How justified is the carefully hedged gloom often

1. Professor T. B. Millar (1970: 93-94) headed a review of seven books on the Commonwealth "Empire into Commonwealth into History," although he did remark that

AUTHOR'S NOTE: An early version of this article was prepared while the author enjoyed the facilities of the Center for Commonwealth and Comparative Studies of Duke

INTERNATIONAL STUDIES QUARTERLY, Vol. 25 No. 3, September 1981 469-490
© 1981 I.S.A.

expressed over the Commonwealth? This article considers the importance of the Commonwealth from the point of view of its most vital constituents, the heads of government at the apex of the foreign policy-making structure in each member state. Using their participation in the periodic Prime Ministers/Heads of Government meetings[2] as an indicator, it suggests that the Commonwealth remains of greater, although not unreduced, relevance and importance to its members than many of its best friends have been prepared to believe.

With the major exception of M. Margaret Ball's excellent *The "Open" Commonwealth* (1971: v), the "basic premise" of which is

---

"it is still too early to write the obituary." Professor J.D.B. Miller (1974: 525) subtitled the third of the authoritative Chatham House Commonwealth surveys "Problems of Expansion and Attrition" and concluded that "it would be an irony if the Commonwealth and la Francophonie existed amicably side by side as primarily cultural bodies flourishing on what had been taught in the schools of empire." Reviewing Miller's volume, Lord Garner (1974: 205) observed that in view of such problems as war between India and Pakistan, the 1964 East African army mutinies, and the Nigerian civil war, "it was hardly remarkable that alike in Britain, the Dominions and in the newer Commonwealth countries, the fires of enthusiasm for the Commonwealth ceased to burn with the same intensity." Lionel Elvin (1974: 109) expressed the fear that "unless more is done in the next few years to make the Commonwealth a reality in the minds of its young people it will probably fade away, as its critics have often said it would." In the view of S. A. de Smith (1971: 360) "ten years hence we may be looking back wistfully in the knowledge that the Commonwealth of 1970 was the best available cheshire cat." The metamorphosis of the *Journal of Commonwealth Political Studies* into *Journal of Commonwealth and Comparative Politics* in 1973 and the renaming of Duke University's Center for Commonwealth Studies to the Center for Commonwealth and Comparative Studies in 1976 also suggest lack of faith in the future of the Commonwealth.

2. The designation "Prime Ministers Meeting," deriving from the earlier meetings when all delegations were led by prime ministers, became less appropriate in the 1960s as several Commonwealth member states turned to presidential or military forms of government. In the final communiqué of the 1964 meeting the phrase "meeting of Commonwealth Heads of Government" was used on page 9. By the 1969 meeting it had moved up to page 1. The new name appeared in the title of the final communiqué of the 1971 meeting and has been used consistently since.

University and subsequently presented at the 1978 Australasian Political Studies Association Conference. I have benefited from the comments of colleagues along the way and from two generations of editors and reviewers of this journal. Constraints of space prevent many of the additional analyses, correlations, and comparisons which have been suggested. While all assistance, including the cooperation of the Commonwealth Secretariat in providing data, is gratefully acknowledged, both blame and responsibility rest with the author.

"that the contemporary relationships among Commonwealth countries are essentially those to be found within international organizations of a traditional sort, and are no longer of a constitutional nature despite the fact that certain Commonwealth nations retain constitutional links with Britain," the Commonwealth has remained outside the mainstream of analysis of international organization.[3] Professor J.D.B. Miller (1974: 518-519) explains that the "contemporary study of international organization . . . [is] . . . very much the preserve of American scholars" and suggests that "it has produced little or nothing about the Commonwealth or bodies which might be compared with it" because of preoccupation with the United Nations system, alliances, integration, and regional organizations, within which categories the Commonwealth fits with difficulty.[4]

Most scholarship on the Commonwealth has been in the British tradition, which means that it is thorough and highly literate but also means that the Commonwealth has not been subjected to systematic quantitative and behavioral study. The dearth of more scientifically oriented studies stems in part from the nature of the organization. Scientism flourishes where the data are easiest and cheapest to obtain (Malitza, 1977: 140). The Commonwealth's more interesting activities take place *in camera* or at least out of the limelight. There are no votes which would lend themselves to voting and bloc analysis. Techniques such as formal content analysis, aggregate data analysis, systematic history, or events-data analysis have apparently not been applied to the Commonwealth. This essay makes a modest beginning at the quantitative study of the Commonwealth by focusing on one aspect of Commonwealth behavior, participation in the periodic Prime Ministers/Heads of Government meetings, the right of attendance being the hallmark of Commonwealth membership.

3. Studies of the Commonwealth Secretariat also treat the Commonwealth as an international organization. See, for example, Ingram (1975) and Leach (1971).

4. Robert Jackson (1974: 362) has pointed out that as "an attempt to give a durable institutional expression to the diffusion around the world of values, instincts, and assumptions of a particular tradition," the Commonwealth is analogous with, for example, the Arab League, the Russian-led "Socialist Commonwealth," or Francophonie. The analogy has yet to receive the attention it deserves.

No pretense is made that this captures the essence of Commonwealth development over three decades. It complements rather than substitutes for the body of fine traditional writing on the Commonwealth.

The analysis rests on an interlocking set of assumptions. States themselves do not make foreign policy decisions and act upon them. Decisions are made by individuals in decision-making roles, ultimately by the head of government. What is important to a state is what is perceived as important by individuals in decision-making roles. The result of decision-making is the allocation of resources. Resources allocated in the foreign policy decision-making process are various and multitudinous, but important among them are personnel and time. There is perhaps no allocatable resource more precious to a head of government than time. How he chooses to allocate his time is therefore an indicator of what he perceives as important. If he perceives an international summit conferencing system[5] as important, he will exert himself to attend its meetings; if he does not, he is less likely to make the effort. If he is confronted with several international summit conferences in the course of a year, as most Commonwealth heads of government are, the sessions he chooses to attend personally will reflect an assessment of the relative importance of the organizations or conferencing systems involved.

It should be stressed that the utility of this approach depends upon the analysis of as large a body of data for as long a time span as possible and conclusions must be drawn from trends and patterns. Individual instances of nonparticipation by a head of government in an international conference may indeed be attributable to compelling personal circumstance. Not all illnesses are diplomatic. However, it is assumed that over time

5. By "summit conference" is meant any international conference at which the norm is that states eligible to attend will be represented by the individual at the apex of their governmental hierarchy. An "international summit conferencing system" refers to a set of states, which may but need not constitute a formal international organization, which meet together at the summit level on a recurrent basis. The usage here differs from that stipulated elsewhere. For example, Galtung (1964: 36) defines "as a summit meeting *any ad hoc meeting of heads of state, heads of government and/or foreign ministers where at least two of the big powers are represented*" (emphasis in the original).

instances of ill health and similar considerations are randomly distributed and that any patterns which present themselves are the result of acts of volition. Application of this approach presents behaviorally derived and objective answers to some of the questions which have often been asked, if only implicitly, about the Commonwealth and answered intuitively.

Data Base

Attendance data were compiled for each of the 22 Commonwealth Prime Ministers/Heads of Government meetings starting with the first in 1944 and continuing through the most recent in 1979.[6] Data were compiled only for full members. "Special members" Nauru and Tuvalu are excluded and such anomalies as the presence by invitation and not by right of Indian and Southern Rhodesian delegations in 1944 and of the prime minister of the Federation of Rhodesia and Nyasaland through 1963 are ignored. In each case it was recorded whether the member state was represented by its head of government (designated "H" in the tables which follow), underrepresented (designated "U"), or absent (designated "A"). No distinction was made between prime ministers and the presidents, chairpersons of the national liberation councils, supreme military commanders, and so on who turned up with increasing frequency after 1960 as the independence constitutions of the new states gave way to presidential forms or military rule. The important question in each case was whether or not the state was in fact represented by the effective head of government.[7] For the 1944-1965 and 1977-1979 meetings, data derive from press accounts. For other

6. The 1952 Commonwealth Economic Conference is excluded. Although it was attended by six of the then eight Commonwealth prime ministers, it "does not rank as a Prime Ministers meeting in the opinion of the Commonwealth Relations Office" (Miller, 1965: 69).

7. A useful starting point in making this determination was *Bidwell's Guide to Government Ministers*, Vol. III: *The British Empire and Successor States 1900-1972* (Bidwell, 1974).

sessions, information came from each meeting's "Directory of Delegations" in the files of the Commonwealth Secretariat at Marlborough House. Similar sources were used to compile attendance data for other international summit conferences in which Commonwealth states participated.

In order to code a simple "H," "U," or "A" for each member state for each meeting, certain conventions were adopted. On those rare occasions where a head of government arrived, left, or was deposed during a meeting, an "H" was recorded. Representation by an acting prime minister was coded "U." Two cases where states did not officially participate in meetings although their representatives were unofficially on the scene were coded "A."

The Prime Ministers/Heads of Government Meetings

The periodic meeting of heads of government is the most salient symbol of the contemporary Commonwealth. The crown is physically distant and its relevance increasingly obscure for the growing number of Commonwealth member states which have abandoned dominion for republic status and whose populations no longer receive daily reminders of their historical links with the monarchy on their postage stamps and coinage. The Commonwealth Secretariat, in existence since 1966, is remote and not much in the public eye. The Prime Ministers/Heads of Government meeting is in the news when it occurs and domestic coverage of each member's delegation underscores that country's membership.

The present series of Commonwealth summits began with a session convened in London in 1944 by Winston Churchill as "a continuation and culmination, of the specifically personal contacts he had established and maintained with other Commonwealth leaders throughout the War" (Normanbrook, 1964: 248).[8]

8. Lord Normanbrook, in his former capacity as Secretary of the United Kingdom Cabinet, was responsible for arrangements for some of the earlier meetings and his brief article is a useful insider's account of the origins and procedures of the meetings. The rich body of memoirs by participants in the earlier meetings was drawn upon extensively by the

To date there have been 22 Prime Ministers/Heads of Government meetings, some details of which are summarized in Table 1.

The hallmark of the meetings has been their informality. At the earliest meetings, there were no prearranged agenda, no delivery of set speeches, no formal votes, no formal resolutions, no published verbatim proceedings. Sessions were held in the intimacy of the Cabinet Room at 10 Downing Street and the consensus which emerged during the meeting was expressed in a final communiqué. As membership increased, meetings began to exhibit some of the characteristics of more orthodox international organizations. As early as 1962, the final communiqué was supplemented by "regular press handouts of major speeches" (Robinson, 1966: 116) and there was a growing use of set speeches intended as much for external as internal effect. At the Singapore meeting of 1971, there was a conscious effort to recover something of the earlier informality. There were "at least one or two meetings almost *in camera* without advisors" and "Prime Minister Lee, who chaired the conference, spent much of his time urging participants to table their documents and not read them"; by the 1973 Ottawa meeting participants were "arguing cases" rather than "reading statements at each other" (Trudeau, 1974: 40). There were still no formal votes or resolutions and the essential nature of the meetings as an opportunity for personal exchanges among heads of government continued to be evidenced in the absence of preparatory gatherings of foreign ministers to prepare agenda and draft resolutions for subsequent endorsement at the summit level.

As is evident from Table 1, scheduling of the meetings has been erratic. Intervals between meetings have ranged from six months to nearly three years, although since 1969 a pattern of a roughly two-year interval has emerged. In earlier years, each meeting dispersed without setting the time or place for the next, leaving this to be decided by need (in practice "need" as interpreted by Great Britain). "By 1964 charges were being made by the newer members that Britain was manipulating the Com-

---

late Trevor Reese in "The Conference System" (1971). The meetings are also covered in more general treatments of the Commonwealth. See Ball, 1971: 37-49; Miller, 1974: 393-397, 1965: 67-71.

TABLE 1

Attendance at Commonwealth Prime Ministers/Heads of Government Meetings, 1944-1979

Year	Dates	Venue	Duration	Members	Aggregate Attendance						Old States			New States			Dominions[a]			Local Monarchies			Republics		
					A		U		H		Total	H		Total	H		Total	H		Total	H		Total	H	
					n	%	n	%	n	%		n	%		n	%		n	%		n	%		n	%
1944	May 1-16	London	16 days	5	0	0	0	0	5	100	5	5	100	0	0	0	5	5	100	0			0		
1946	April 23-May 8; May 20-23	London	20	5	0	0	1	20	4	80	5	4	80	0	0	0	5	4	80	0			0		
1948	October 11-22	London	12	8	0	0	2	25	6	75	5	3	60	3	3	100	8	6	75	0			0		
1949	April 22-27	London	6	8	0	0	1	13	7	88	5	4	80	3	3	100	8	7	87	0			0		
1951	January 4-12	London	9	8	0	0	0	0	8	100	5	5	100	3	3	100	7	7	100	0			1	1	100
1953	June 3-9	London	7	8	0	0	0	0	8	100	5	5	100	3	3	100	7	7	100	0			1	1	100
1955	January 31-February 8	London	9	8	0	0	1	13	7	88	5	4	80	3	3	100	7	6	86	0			2	2	100
1956	June 27-July 6	London	10	8	0	0	0	0	8	100	5	5	100	3	3	100	6	6	100	0			2	2	100
1957	June 26-July 5	London	10	9	0	0	3	33	6	67	5	3	60	4	3	75	7	4	57	0			2	2	100
1960	May 3-13	London	11	10	0	0	2	20	8	80	5	4	80	5	4	80	7	5	71	1	1	100	2	2	100
1961	March 8-17	London	10	12	0	0	2	20	10	83	5	5	100	7	5	73	7	7	100	1	0	0	4	3	75
1962	September 10-19	London	10	15	0	0	3	20	12	80	4	4	100	11	8	79	10	9	90	1	1	100	6	4	67
1964	July 8-15	London	8	18	0	0	3	17	15	83	4	4	100	14	11	76	11	10	91	1	1	100	8	6	75
1965	June 10-17	London	8	21	0	0	4	19	17	81	4	4	100	17	13	73	12	10	83	1	1	100	9	3	33
1966	January 11-12	Lagos	2	22	3	14	9	41	10	45	4	2	50	18	8	44	12	9	90	1	0	0	10	3	30
1966	September 6-15	London	10	23	1	4	9	39	13	57	4	4	100	19	9	58	12	10	91	1	1	100	10	3	30
1969	January 7-15	London	9	28	0	0	4	14	24	86	4	4	100	24	20	83	13	13	100	3	3	100	12	8	67
1971	January 14-22	Singapore	9	31	0	0	6	19	25	81	4	4	100	27	21	78	12	10	83	5	5	100	14	10	71
1973	August 2-10	Ottawa	9	32	0	0	10	31	22	69	4	4	100	28	18	64	11	9	82	5	5	100	16	8	50
1975	April 29-May 6	Kingston	8	33	0	0	5	15	28	85	4	4	100	29	24	83	11	10	91	5	5	100	17	13	76
1977	June 8-15	London	8	35	2	6	7	20	26	74	4	4	100	31	22	71	11	11	100	5	5	100	19	10	53
1979	August 1-7	Lusaka	7	39	0	0	12	31	27	69	4	4	100	35	23	66	13	12	92	5	1	20	21	14	67
											Average 90%			Average 73%			Average 86%			Average 83%			Average 64%		

NOTE: All percentages rounded to the nearest whole percent.   a. Including Great Britain.

A = absent; U = underrepresented; H = represented by head of government.

monwealth to its own ends—even that Britain was trying to time
Commonwealth conferences and adapt agenda to suit the domestic political situation, particularly in relation to the Rhodesian
situation" (Ingram, 1975: 141). The convoking of a Prime
Ministers meeting in Lagos in January 1966 at the behest of the
Nigerian Prime Minister to discuss the Rhodesian unilateral
declaration of independence and the establishment of the Commonwealth Secretariat in the same year prevented future meetings from appearing to be British initiatives. The current practice
is for each meeting to agree upon the time and place of the next.
Although as early as 1949 there was talk of rotating the meetings
among Commonwealth capitals, 17 of the 22 meetings have been
held in London.

Duration of the meetings ranged from two to twenty days, with
a median of 9 and a mean of 9.5 days. The three shorter meetings
were those convened for a single purpose. The six-day 1949
meeting was held solely to discuss India's pending constitutional
change from dominion to republic; the seven-day 1953 session
convened in the immediate wake of the coronation of Queen
Elizabeth II which had brought all the prime ministers to London
anyway; and the two-day meeting in Lagos in January 1966 per-
tained directly to Southern Rhodesia. The Commonwealth Prime
Ministers/Heads of Government meetings tend to be longer than
most major summit conferences which include substantial numbers of Commonwealth heads of government. The average length
of more than nine days for Commonwealth meetings can, for
example, be contrasted with averages of less than six days for
Nonaligned and Organization of African Unity summits.

There will probably be no return to the leisurely pace of the
earlier Prime Ministers meetings: The 1946 session met for a total
of twenty days, excluding an eleven-day recess during which
delegates fanned out over Europe while waiting for Prime
Minister King to arrive by ship from Canada. But eight or nine
days is still a long time for a head of government to be away from
his desk. The length of the Commonwealth meetings enables
them to work more effectively than more frenetic gatherings,
thereby perhaps causing eligible participants to value them more

highly. However, their length also means greater demands on time. That the Commonwealth meetings seem to be settling down into a biennial pattern is not necessarily a mitigating circumstance, for it may be easier for a head of government to spare four or five days every year than to find a larger block of time less frequently.

Has the Commonwealth Declined in Importance?

Several things stand out from the aggregate attendance data for the 22 meetings presented in Table 1. Attendance by heads of government ranged from 100% on five occasions to a low of 45% at the special session on Rhodesia in January 1966. Level of attendance seems to be responsive to and indicative of the Commonwealth in crisis. The 1957 meeting, attended by 67% of the heads of government (the lowest percentage up to that time), was the first to be held after Britain had incurred the displeasure of both old and new Commonwealth states through its participation with France and Israel in the invasion of Suez. The nadir of attendance reached at the 1966 meetings reflects dissatisfaction over Britain's handling of the Rhodesian unilateral declaration of independence of November 1965, and suggests that the Commonwealth was still viewed by many of its members as a grouping within which Britain remained at least *primus inter pares.*

Not only did the Rhodesian crisis coincide with the lowest levels of attendance to date, but it produced the first absences. Tanzania, Ghana, and Australia boycotted the first 1966 meeting, although for different reasons. Tanzania and Ghana had broken diplomatic relations with Britain over Britain's failure to end Rhodesia's unilateral declaration of independence, by force if necessary, and contended that nothing could be gained from further talking in Lagos. Australia stayed away, said Prime Minister Menzies, because the "conference could do no more than expose great differences and create much bitterness." Tanzania was absent from the second 1966 meeting in London for the same reason as from the first in Lagos.

After 1966, there were no further absences until the 1977 London meeting when there were two for unrelated reasons.

Uganda went unrepresented in 1977 after Great Britain's Prime Minister Callaghan, to the distress of several African Commonwealth states which saw this as an unhappy precedent, made it abundantly and publicly clear that Ugandan President Idi Amin would not be welcome as the leader of his country's delegation. (Amin, who came to power through a coup while President Obote was attending the 1971 Commonwealth meeting in Singapore, had not attended any previous meetings but had sent representatives.) Seychelles President Mancham, in London to attend the first Commonwealth meeting since his country had become independent, was overthrown by a coup. He was not permitted to take the Seychelles' seat in the meeting and the new government did not send a delegation.

The aggregate attendance data give some credence to a decline in the importance of the Commonwealth as perceived by its member states. 100% attendance by eligible heads of government was the exception rather than the rule even when membership was small, but it did not occur at all after 1961. If attendance by heads of government (H) is averaged for successive groupings of seven meetings prior to 1979, thereby smoothing out fluctuations, a decline in level of attendance is apparent:

1944-1955	H = 90%
1956-1965	H = 84%
1966-1977	H = 73%
1979	H = 69%

However, while level of attendance has been on the decline, the decline has not been of catastrophic proportions. Moreover, the dearth of absences suggests that participation in the Commonwealth continues to be valued highly.

Is The Commonwealth Less Important to New Members than to Old?

The old Commonwealth states are the white-ruled states which were represented at the first Prime Ministers meeting (Great

Britain, Australia, Canada, New Zealand, and, until its withdrawal in 1961, South Africa) and which have close cultural and historical bonds, including common recognition of the English monarch as head of state. The new members are Asian, African, Mediterranean, Pacific, and Caribbean states which gained independence from Britain after World War II. Participation in Commonwealth Prime Ministers/Heads of Government meetings by heads of government of old Commonwealth and new Commonwealth states is presented in Table 1.

Through 1961, the still small number of new Commonwealth states recorded levels of participation higher than or equal to the old Commonwealth states. After 1961, the old Commonwealth heads of government became more regular in their attendance, showing 100% participation except at the special session on Southern Rhodesia in January 1966, which Australia boycotted and to which New Zealand sent only a high commissioner. At the same time the number of new Commonwealth states increased rapidly and their average level of attendance declined. The pattern can be seen more readily if averages are again computed for seven-meeting groups:

1944-1955 H for Old States = 86%   H for New States = 100%
1956-1965 H for Old States = 91%   H for New States = 80%
1966-1977 H for Old States = 93%   H for New States = 69%
1979   H for Old States = 100%   H for New States = 66%

The new Commonwealth states are responsible for the decline in level of attendance. In fact, the decline in level of attendance by new states was greater than the decline apparent from the aggregate attendance figures, for it was partially compensated for by the old states. According to the indicator employed here, Commonwealth membership has come to be of more importance to old than to new Commonwealth states. Nevertheless, the average level of participation by new states in the Commonwealth meetings remains high when compared to some other conferencing systems, as will be seen. Eleven new Commonwealth states (Bahamas, Bangladesh, Barbados, Botswana, Grenada, Kiribati,

Mauritius, Papua-New Guinea, Singapore, Solomon Islands, and Tonga) have recorded 100% attendance at the summit level, a record matched only by Britain among the old states.

Is the Commonwealth Less Important to
New Commonwealth States than are
Other Summit Conferencing Groups?

If the Commonwealth has declined in the esteem of new Commonwealth states, it might be thought that it would be replaced in their eyes by groupings of greater geographical or ideological relevance. Tables 2 and 3 present attendance data for the six Nonaligned Summit Conferences (1961-1979), which most new Commonwealth states were eligible to attend upon independence, and seventeen sessions of the Assembly of Heads of State and Government of the Organization of African Unity (OAU) (1964-1979), which included every African Commonwealth state. New Commonwealth states participate in a number of other international summit conferencing systems, but these have involved the largest number of new Commonwealth states over the longest period of time.

The Commonwealth more than holds its own against both the Nonaligned group and the OAU, although there were individual Nonaligned and OAU meetings where the level of participation by new Commonwealth states exceeded that at individual Commonwealth meetings. After 1960 the same 25 new Commonwealth states which were represented at Nonaligned conferences on 56% of the possible occasions attended Commonwealth Prime Ministers/Heads of Government meetings at the head of government level 70% of the time. Commonwealth participation in OAU meetings was still lower. The same fourteen African states which were represented at the head of government level at OAU sessions 46% of the time were represented at the head of government level 70% of the time at Commonwealth Prime Ministers/Heads of Government meetings.

The Commonwealth, according to the indicator used here, has remained more important to new Commonwealth states than

TABLE 2

Attendance by New Commonwealth States at
Nonaligned Conferences

Conference	All Invited States			Commonwealth States		
	Total	H n	%	Total	H n	%
Belgrade 1961	27	21	78	5	4	80
Cairo 1964	66	30	45	13	5	38
Lusaka 1970	65	25	38	21	11	52
Algiers 1973	76	58	76	23	17	74
Colombo 1976	85	42	49	25	14	56
Havana 1979	94	49	52	25	12	48
		Average	54%		Average	56%

NOTE: All percentages rounded to the nearest whole percent.
H = head of government.

TABLE 3

Attendance by New Commonwealth States at OAU Assemblies
of Heads of State and Government

Session	All OAU Members			Commonwealth States		
	Total	H n	%	Total	H n	%
Cairo 1964	34	24	71	7	7	100
Accra 1965	36	17	47	9	7	78
Addis Ababa 1966	38	17	45	11	6	55
Kinshasa 1967	38	18	47	11	4	36
Algiers 1968	40	24	60	13	6	46
Addis Ababa 1969	41	16	39	13	6	46
Addis Ababa 1970	41	17	41	13	8	62
Addis Ababa 1971	41	10	24	13	3	23
Rabat 1972	41	20	49	13	4	31
Addis Ababa 1973	41	28	68	13	8	62
Mogadiscio 1974	42	27	64	13	8	62
Kampala 1975	46	19	41	13	2	15
Addis Ababa 1976	46	12	26	13	5	38
Port Louis 1976	48	10	21	14	5	36
Libreville 1977	49	22	45	14	6	43
Khartoum 1978	49	29	59	14	6	43
Monrovia 1979	49	26	53	14	7	50
		Average	47%		Average	46%

NOTE: All percentages rounded to the nearest whole percent.
H = head of government.

have either the Organization of African Unity or the Nonaligned movement. Moreover, the aggregate attendance figures of Tables 2 and 3 suggest that the Commonwealth is doing well indeed in drawing an average of 73% of the eligible heads of government of new Commonwealth states, while the OAU is able to achieve an average of only 47% and the Nonaligned movement 54% attendance by eligible heads of government.

Comparison of Commonwealth, Nonaligned, and OAU summit attendance sheds light on the priorities and behavior of individual states and their heads. States with lowest levels of participation in the Commonwealth meetings also record low levels of participation in the other summit conferencing systems. Excluding Dominica and St. Lucia (recent Commonwealth members which were underrepresented at the sole meeting they have been eligible to attend), only three states have been represented at Commonwealth meetings by their heads of government less than 50% of the time: Kenya, 20% (2 out of 10); Trinidad and Tobago, 36% (4 out of 11); and Ghana, 43% (6 out of 14). In the case of Kenya it might be tempting to infer a relationship between the physical attack experienced by President Jomo Kenyatta in the streets of London during the first Commonwealth meeting after Kenya's independence and his subsequent nonattendance. However, Kenyatta also absented himself from all four Nonaligned and all but one of fifteen OAU summits he was eligible to attend. In his case a general pattern of nonattendance reflects ill health, advancing age, and a resulting disinclination to travel abroad. Dr. Eric Williams of Trinidad and Tobago, who attended but one of five possible Nonaligned summits, also emerges as a nonenthusiast for summit meetings. Ghana's first head of government, Kwame Nkrumah, recorded high levels of attendance at meetings of each system, but after his downfall in the 1966 Ghana coup, the domestic preoccupations of Ghana's successive military and civilian regimes brought the averages for the Nonaligned and OAU summits down to 50% (3 out of 6) and 35% (6 out of 17) respectively.

While a low level of Commonwealth participation predicts a low level of participation in Nonaligned and OAU summits, the converse does not hold true. Eight Commonwealth states, excluding the habitually underrepresented Kenya, Ghana, and Trinidad and Tobago, were represented at the Nonaligned summits at the head of government level 50% or less of the possible occasions (Gambia and Malawi, 0%; Nigeria, 17%; Malaysia, 40%; Jamaica, Mauritius, Singapore, Swaziland, 50%). Each of these was represented at the summit level at Commonwealth meetings more than 50% of the time (Mauritius and Singapore, 100%; Gambia, 89%; Swaziland, 83%; Malawi, 80%; Malaysia, 77%; Jamaica, 64%; Nigeria, 58%). The same pattern emerges with the OAU. Again excluding Kenya and Ghana, there were seven states which registered less than 50% attendance by a head of government at OAU meetings (Malawi, 12%; Seychelles, 25%; Swaziland, 31%; Lesotho, 33%; Botswana, 40%; Mauritius, 46%; Sierra Leone, 47%). Each of these recorded 50% or higher representation at the summit level at Commonwealth meetings (Botswana, Mauritius, 100%; Sierra Leone, 91%; Lesotho, Swaziland, 83%; Malawi, 80%; Seychelles, 50%).This suggests that certain states demonstrate a marked preference for the Commonwealth over the Nonaligned or OAU meetings. The following sections consider two factors which such states may have in common.

Does Republic Status Matter?

When India, which had become independent as a dominion with a British governor-general representing the crown as head of state, decided to become a republic there was a constitutional crisis for the Commonwealth. The 1949 Prime Ministers meeting, convened solely to consider the problem posed by India's proposed change of status, arrived at a formula whereby India could continue as a member by acknowledging the king as the symbol of the free association of the Commonwealth and as its head. To some this was the end of the unique and essential closeness which bound the Commonwealth together, but subsequently Commonwealth membership for republics became commonplace. By 1979, fourteen new Commonwealth states which had become independent as dominions had made the transition to republic and there were seven new Commonwealth states which had achieved independence and Commonwealth membership as republics without an intervening period of dominion status. The four remaining old Commonwealth states and nine new Commonwealth states still recognized the crown as head of state. Five new Commonwealth states were local monarchies, recognizing an indigenous royal ruler as head of state.

Commonwealth Prime Ministers / Heads of Government meeting attendance figures for the three constitutional types presented in Table 1 suggest that there is some basis for fears that inclusion of republics would weaken the Commonwealth. The growing number of republics after 1961 corresponded with the decrease in attendance by heads of government. Every meeting after 1961 was attended by a higher percentage of eligible dominion heads of government than republic heads of government. It is also noteworthy that the heads of government of local monarchies registered a higher average level of attendance than did those of republics. Table 4 compares Commonwealth attendance before and after the achievement of republic status for those states which made the transition after independence. For twelve of the fourteen states, level of participation declined after the change to republic status. This is not, of course, to say that there is a causal relationship between achievement of republic status and a decrease in the importance attached to the Commonwealth. Rather, the change to republic status can be seen as symptomatic of other changes and preoccupations which widen the distance between new Commonwealth states and their colonial bonds with Great Britain and other members of the Commonwealth.

Is the Commonwealth More Important to the
First Generation Heads of Government of New Commonwealth
States than to Subsequent Generations?

In almost every instance, the first generation leaders of the new Commonwealth states emerged from the British system and could be expected to share the values frequently articulated if not

TABLE 4

Attendance of New Commonwealth States Before and
After Transition to Republic Status

Member	Meetings Eligible to Attend as Dominion			Meetings Eligible to Attend as Republic		
	Total	H n	%	Total	H n	%
Gambia	4	4	100	5	4	80
Ghana	2	2	100	12	4	33
Guyana	3	3	100	4	2	50
India	2	2	100	18	12	67
Kenya	1	1	100	9	1	11
Malawi	3	3	100	7	5	71
Malta	6	6	100	3	2	67
Nigeria	2	2	100	10	5	50
Pakistan	5	5	100	11	7	64
Sierra Leone	7	6	86	4	4	100
Sri Lanka	16	10	63	4	3	75
Tanzania	1	1	100	10	7	70
Trinidad and Tobago	9	4	44	2	0	0
Uganda	4	4	100	6	3	50
		Average	82%		Average	56%

NOTE: All percentages rounded to the nearest whole percent.
H = head of government.

always practiced in the Commonwealth. While they had fought
for independence, the fight had been waged with British ideas
through British institutions. The first generation leaders had a
continuing commitment to the Commonwealth if for no other
reason than that it was their decision to keep their states in the
Commonwealth after independence. In their first-hand experience with and attachment to the values associated with the
Commonwealth, the first generation of new Commonwealth
heads of government often, although not always, differs from the
second and subsequent generations, especially where the subsequent generation came to power through extraconstitutional
means. It might be expected, then, that post-first generation
heads of government would evidence less enthusiasm for the
Commonwealth.

TABLE 5

Attendance by First and Subsequent Generation Heads of
Government of New Commonwealth States

| | First Generation | | | Subsequent Generation | | | | | |
| | | | | In Office by Con- stitutional Means | | | In Office by Extra- constitutional Means | | |
	Total	Attending n	%	Total	Attending n	%	Total	Attending n	%
1948 London	3	3	100	0			0		
1949 London	3	3	100	0			0		
1951 London	2	2	100	1	1	100	0		
1953 London	1	1	100	2	2	100	0		
1955 London	1	1	100	2	2	100	0		
1956 London	1	1	100	2	2	100	0		
1957 London	2	2	100	2	1	50	0		
1960 London	3	3	100	1	0	0	1	1	100
1961 London	5	5	100	1	1	100	1	1	100
1962 London	9	7	78	1	0	0	1	1	100
1964 London	10	8	80	3	2	67	1	1	100
1965 London	13	10	77	3	2	67	1	1	100
1966 Lagos	14	7	50	3	1	33	1	0	0
1966 London	13	8	62	3	1	33	3	0	0
1969 London	17	16	94	4	4	100	3	0	0
1971 Singapore	19	17	89	6	4	67	2	0	0
1973 Ottawa	19	12	63	6	5	83	3	1	33
1975 Kingston	20	17	85	6	6	100	3	1	33
1977 London	19	15	79	7	6	86	5	1	20
1979 Lusaka	18	13	72	11	6	55	6	4	67
		Average	79%		Average	72%		Average	39%

NOTE: All percentages rounded to the nearest whole percent.

Commonwealth meeting attendance data for first and subsequent generations of new Commonwealth heads of government
are presented in Table 5. Prior to 1964, the number of second
generation leaders was so small as to render any generalization
extremely suspect; and even in 1979, 18 of the 35 new Commonwealth states still had the same individual as head of government
as when they became independent. The situation varied from
meeting to meeting, but on average, 79% of eligible first
generation heads of government attended the meetings, while
61% of the subsequent generations of heads of government

attended. Within the group of post-first generation heads of government, an average of 72% of those who had come to power through constitutional means attended, an average not substantially lower than for the first generation. Personal attendance of post-first generation heads of government who came to power through extraconstitutional means averaged a much lower 39% of the time. A combination of domestic political preoccupations and lack of affinity for the Commonwealth perhaps accounts for this low attendance rate.

Conclusion

The behavioral indicator employed here suggests a Commonwealth more important to the leaders of its constituent member states, including the new Commonwealth states, than might have been predicted on the basis of subjective literature on the Commonwealth. There has been a decline in attendance by heads of government at the Prime Ministers/Heads of Government meetings, but the decline has not been of catastrophic proportions. Moreover, according to the indicator used, the Commonwealth has been more important than the Organization of African Unity or the Nonaligned movement, which might have been thought to have greater relevance for the states concerned.

Questions can be raised about the utility and validity of the indicator. Does it in fact reveal anything worth knowing? If a head of government is more likely to attend a Commonwealth than a Nonaligned or OAU summit, does this reflect a careful assessment of the importance of the respective conferencing systems, or is it because London offers better dental facilities than Addis Ababa or Havana? Is it because the Commonwealth offers the opportunity to play in a different league, a refreshing change from the OAU and Nonaligned meetings with their endless and repetitive discussions and resolutions on very important but very intractable problems? Is the Commonwealth important to the new states because it is a source of foreign aid? Why have the heads of government of old Commonwealth states become so regular in their attendance? Is it force of habit, or are there diplomatic and economic payoffs?

Although simple level of attendance data do not answer these questions, it can still be argued that the indicator is a useful one. In the first place, the very fact of level of attendance is important. A high level of attendance by heads of government, for whatever reason, is a necessary although not sufficient condition for a successful summit conferencing system. In the second place, where the indicator reveals departures from what was anticipated, it points to questions about the importance of the Commonwealth to its member states which should be explored in greater depth.

If there is no immediate cause for despondence about the health of the Commonwealth, there are trends which merit attention. More new Commonwealth states are moving in the direction of republic status and it is not impossible that one or two of the old Commonwealth states will also undertake this transformation. In the past, transition to republic status has been associated with a decrease in level of participation in the Commonwealth meetings. The first generation of new Commonwealth heads of government continues to die off or otherwise be replaced by individuals who lack the same personal commitment to the Commonwealth. If it is the case that "the future of the meetings of Prime Ministers is the future of the Commonwealth itself" (Miller, 1965: 70), a close watch over attendance patterns at future meetings will be a good means of monitoring the health of the system. When anomalies are detected, their causes can be sought through more narrowly focused means.

Date of receipt of final manuscript: May 4, 1981

REFERENCES

BALL, M. M. (1971) The "Open" Commonwealth. Durham, NC: Duke Univ. Press.
BIDWELL, R. [ed.] (1974) Bidwell's Guide to Government Ministers, Vol. III: The British Empire and Successor States 1900-1972. London: Frank Cass.
DE SMITH, S. A. (1971) "Fundamental rules forty years on." Int. J. 24 (Spring): 347-360.

ELVIN, L. (1974) "Teaching the Commonwealth to the Commonwealth." The Round Table 253 (January): 109-116.

GALTUNG, J. (1964) "Summit meetings and international relations." J. of Peace Research 1: 36-54.

GARNER (1974) "The Commonwealth under strain." The Round Table 253 (January): 205.

INGRAM, D. (1975) "Ten turbulent years: the Commonwealth Secretariat at work." The Round Table 258 (April): 139-148.

JACKSON, R. (1974) "The question of Commonwealth values." The Round Table 256 (October): 359-367

LEACH, R. H. (1971) "The Secretariat." Int. J. 26 (Spring): 374-400.

MALITZA, M. (1977) "Quantification." Int. Social Sci. J. 29, 1: 131-148.

MILLAR, T. B. (1970) "Empire into Commonwealth into history." Int. Organization 24 (Winter): 93-100

MILLER, J.D.B. (1974) Survey of Commonwealth Affairs: Problems of Expansion and Attrition 1953-1969. London: Oxford Univ. Press.

——— (1965) The Commonwealth in the World. Cambridge MA: Harvard Univ. Press.

NORMANBROOK (1964) "Meetings of Commonwealth Prime Ministers." J. of the Parliaments of the Commonwealth 45 (July): 248-254.

REESE, T. (1971) "The conference system." Int. J. 26 (Spring): 361-373.

ROBINSON, K. (1966) "The intergovernmental machinery of Commonwealth consultation and co-operation," in W. B. Hamilton et al. (eds.) A Decade of the Commonwealth 1955-1964. Durham, NC: Duke Univ. Press.

TRUDEAU, P. E. (1974) "The Commonwealth after Ottawa." The Round Table 253 (January): 35-41.

EDITORS' NOTE

The following article is the second in a series of articles translated from the Japanese and published in *International Studies Quarterly* as part of an exchange between the Japan Association of International Relations and the International Studies Association. Its author, Chihiro Hosoya, is President of the Japan Association of International Relations and is a member of the Editorial Board of *International Studies Quarterly*. The article first appeared in *Kokusai Seiji* (International Relations), No. 58, 1977, and was selected by the Japanese Association. The second article selected for Japanese publication by a committee of the International Studies Association was "The Logic of International Interactions" by Andrew Scott, which was published by *Kokusai Seiji* in May 1980. We are pleased to be able to share Professor Hosoya's scholarship with an English-speaking audience, and we look forward to more exchanges in the future. The author and the editors are very much indebted to Professor Thomas Burkman of Old Dominion University for his fine translation.

The 1934 Anglo-Japanese
Nonaggression Pact

CHIHIRO HOSOYA

Department of International Relations
Hitotsubashi University (Tokyo)

Although Japan withdrew from the League of Nations in 1933, it did not completely reject the concept of international cooperation. In fact, during 1934, Japan demonstrated great interest in cementing an Anglo-Japanese nonaggression pact. Japan's overtures were well received in Britain and particularly promoted by Chancellor of the Exchequer Neville Chamberlain and Treasury Undersecretary Warren Fisher. In the end, negotiations broke down over the China question, but not until a complex series of communiqués and commissioned studies had been exchanged. The author utilizes recently declassified British diplomatic documents as well as files from the Japanese Foreign Ministry Archives to examine in detail this important chapter of Far Eastern international politics.

INTERNATIONAL STUDIES QUARTERLY, Vol. 25 No. 3, September 1981 491-517
© 1981 I.S.A.

Introduction

In March 1933, Japan announced its intention to withdraw from the League of Nations. Waving the banner of "autonomous diplomacy" and ignoring world opinion as voiced by the League, the island empire set out in bold pursuit of its own China policy. In so doing, Japan opted to dissociate itself from the universal mechanism for sustaining the post-World War I international order. This course of action, however, should not be construed as a complete rejection of international cooperation or the adoption of an isolationist diplomacy.

A subsequent chain of events (a movement within the League for economic sanctions against Japan, the announcement on April 12, 1933 of the abrogation of the Indo-Japanese commercial treaty, and calls for an embargo of Japanese imports in the British dominions) demonstrated to the Japanese the danger facing "autonomous diplomacy." At the same time war with the Soviet Union, a frequent subject of rumor, could not be ruled out in setting a new course of foreign policy.

During the period from Japan's withdrawal from the League to 1936, Japanese diplomacy groped for a new scheme. In place of a system of multilateral cooperation patterned after Wilsonian notions of a "New Diplomacy," a bilateral model harking back to the "Old Diplomacy" became the object of Japan's quest. What options were open to Japan in its search for political accommodation with the powers? Critical scrutiny of Japanese diplomacy in this period reveals three possible formulae. The first was cooperation with the Soviet Union embodied in a Japan-Soviet non-aggression pact. The second was cooperation with Great Britain and the United States based on an Anglo-Japanese (and American-Japanese) nonaggression pact. The third option, actualized in 1936, was cooperation with Germany through an anti-Comintern pact.

The subject of the present study is the little-known second formula, an Anglo-Japanese nonaggression pact. Although the pact is mentioned in such writings as the biography of Neville Chamberlain (Feiling, 1946: 253-254), full-scale research was not feasible prior to the declassification of British diplomatic documents of the period.[1] The present writer had the opportunity to report on the documents' revelations concerning the pact in a paper given at the Japanese Foreign Ministry Archives in October 1974. But at the same time, little research was available and the only published treatment was an article by historian Ann Trotter (1974). Soon after, however, works touching upon the subject were published in rapid succession by Trotter (1975), Stephen Endicott (1975), and Stephen Pelz (1974) of New Zealand, Canada, and the United States respectively. Moreover, Yōichi Kihata (1977) produced a relevant article.

This scholarly activity has deepened knowledge of the design and details of the Anglo-Japanese nonaggression pact and the historical circumstances which evoked it. This article will attempt to break new ground and avoid needless duplication of the aforementioned work. It will seek to establish an analytical framework for Anglo-Japanese-American tripartite relations, and consider the domestic political processes in Japan and England which bore upon their evolution. For its documentary sources, this treatment will rely upon surviving Japanese diplomatic records in addition to British primary materials.

The Chamberlain-Fisher Line

Within the British government, the first figure to appear onstage as an advocate of an Anglo-Japanese nonaggression pact was Chancellor of the Exchequer and Conservative Party chief Neville Chamberlain. (He would later be notorious for his policy of "appeasement" toward Nazi Germany.) At a cabinet meeting on March 14, 1934, Chamberlain pressed for the creation of a national defense posture whose primary aim was to cope with the growing Nazi menace. To this end, he argued the utility of a

1. For a pre-declassification treatment of the 1934 Anglo-Japanese rapprochement, see Watt (1965: 83-89).

concert with Japan in the Far East (Cab. 9(34), 3/14/34, CAB 23/78).[2]

A year earlier, the British government had begun a comprehensive reexamination of the Empire's defense system. The new specter of Nazi power and German rearmament on the continent coupled with the step-up in Japanese military incursions in the Far East gave this study a sense of urgency. In October 1933, the Committee of Imperial Defense assigned the task to its Defense Requirements Subcommittee (DRC) which included Cabinet Secretary Maurice Hankey, Foreign Office Undersecretary Robert Vansittart, and Treasury Undersecretary Warren Fisher.

The problem of naval power emerged in the deliberations on imperial defense. For years, seapower had been the British Empire's mainstay and England's symbol of glory. Now, with changing circumstances in the world and the Empire, what position should be accorded the Royal Navy? How should the military budget be allocated among the Royal Army, Navy, and Air Force? With a naval disarmament conference approaching, these questions were of utmost concern. It must be remembered that Great Britain at this point had not yet recovered from the doldrums of the Great Depression. Not only was the economy unable to bear a large-scale increase in military expenditures, but the political climate demanded a tax cut and renewed measures to reduce government officials' salaries. Finance officials themselves argued for curbing the growth of the naval budget.

The DRC labored four months investigating defense expenditures and the distribution of forces and presented its report in late February 1934. This report began by listing considerations to be given priority in the stationing of troops: (1) the protection of British possessions and interests in the Far East, (2) defense capability in Europe, and (3) the securing of India against Soviet aggression. In other words, the report ranked armed threats to the Empire in the order of Japan, Germany, and the Soviet Union.

---

2. Until otherwise noted, this and all the following cables and memoranda can be found in the archives of the Public Record Office, London.

While the report urged the completion of the Singapore naval base as a means to achieve preparedness against the Japanese threat, it also called for the improvement of relations with Japan and emphasized the need for a policy to restore "our old terms of cordiality and mutual respect with Japan" (2/28/34, CP 64(34), CAB 24/247). The report can thus be seen as the product of a process of accommodation between two lines. Hankey, of the "Imperial faction," promoted the belief that naval strengthening was the first priority in national defense. The counterview was represented by Fisher of the "Treasury faction," who emphasized the importance of the defense of Europe, and by Vansittart who shared Fisher's anxiety over the German threat.

Chamberlain's proposal for an Anglo-Japanese nonaggression pact was made at a cabinet meeting where the above DRC report was deliberated. Chamberlain's move can be largely explained by his position as leader of the Treasury faction. He insisted that the most serious danger to Great Britain's security lay in Europe and that planning on distribution of forces must give this threat uppermost consideration. From the standpoint of the nation's economic capacity, a tie with Japan would diminish the need to strengthen the nation's defense posture in Asia. Going beyond economic considerations, he addressed the issue of relations with Japan and the United States. "The termination of the Anglo-Japanese Alliance . . . had been a great blow to their amour propre" and an impediment to the development of Anglo-Japanese relations, he said. As for the coming disarmament conference, the United States was seeking British backing in its opposition to alteration of the Japanese naval ratio. If Britain simply aligned itself with the American position, Japanese emotions would be hardened and the situation would be like "pulling the chestnuts out of the fire for them" (Cab. 9(34), 3/14/34, CAB 23/78).

Chamberlain in this period is regarded as pro-Japanese and anti-American (Watt, 1965: 90-92). Without doubt Chamberlain's espousal of an Anglo-Japanese nonaggression pact sprang not only from financial considerations but also from the desire to reduce trade-related economic friction between Britain and

Japan. A concealed motive was the search for understanding with Japan on the China issue. Moreover, one can detect in Chamberlain the emotional elements of antagonism toward the United States and nostalgia for the age of the Anglo-Japanese Alliance. In Treasury there was one man—Undersecretary Fisher—who understood and affirmed Chamberlain's approach to the international situation and Britain's defense needs. One could surmise that Fisher was the prime mover behind the Japan concert line. The emotional element in the pro-Japanese and anti-American views expressed in his memoranda is more intense than Chamberlain's. His anti-American posture is revealed, for instance, in an April 19, 1934 memorandum on naval arms limitation:

> The very last thing in the world that we can count on is American support; . . . a naval agreement between ourselves and the United States is the most complete non sequitur from any and every point of view. . . . We gave up a completely satisfactory treaty with Japan for a completely unsatisfactory naval Pact of Washington. . . . We should effect a thorough and lasting accommodation with the Japanese.[3]

The policy of British cooperation with Japan championed by Chamberlain and Fisher was motivated by economic interests. Anticipated financial advantage, of course, made the policy attractive. Also operating among officials at Treasury was a strong sense of disillusionment with the American attitude toward such issues as war debts. Additionally, behind-the-scenes, subtle influences (which will be explained later) emanated from the financial and industrial circles, and the court.

A majority of those present at a cabinet meeting on March 14 favored Chamberlain's proposal. Navy Minister Bolton Eyres-Monsell registered his approval by saying, "Japan wanted equality in armaments but she might not press this demand if she had a pact of mutual nonaggression with this country." Foreign Secretary John Simon likewise commented that "a nonaggression

---

3. Memorandum by Sir Warren Fisher on defense requirements and naval strategy in Medlicott et al. (eds.) *Documents on British Foreign Policy*, (1973). Hereafter, this volume shall be referred to in the text as simply *DBFP*.

pact would be of advantage to us." But Prime Minister Ramsey MacDonald, who was regarded as a member of the "pro-America faction," voiced misgivings. The pact, he feared, was likely to be viewed by the United States "as an alliance." At the close of that day's meeting, the foreign secretary and the navy minister were assigned the task of bringing to a subsequent cabinet session a concrete proposal for improvement of Anglo-Japanese relations (Cab. 9(34), 3/14/34, CAB 23/78).

The memorandum which Simon submitted to the cabinet on March 16 displayed a negative attitude toward an Anglo-Japanese nonaggression pact. After surveying the pros and cons, the memorandum in sum saw the effects of such a pact as deleterious to Britain's international position. Even were the agreement to be achieved apart from the upcoming naval disarmament negotiations, "it would hardly be useful." The memorandum concluded that if the pact could be used at the disarmament talks as a bargaining tool to induce Japan to withdraw its demand for parity, it would be worth exploring at that time (3/16/34, CP 80(34), CAB 24/248).

This memorandum, an about-face from the foreign secretary's statement two days before, was without doubt a product of thinking among officials of the Foreign Office, especially those of the Far East Department. The previous December, the Far East Department had studied not only all aspects of Anglo-Japanese relations but also British Far Eastern policy. C. W. Orde, Far East Department chief, had concluded on December 14 that there was no need to revise the British policy of impeding the establishment of Manchukuo, and that any scheme to revive the Anglo-Japanese Alliance would risk the danger of a split with the United States. J. T. Pratt, an officer in the department, had declared that arguments for an alliance were marked by emotion rather than reason, and even stated that there was difficulty in cultivating friendship with "the most ego-centric race on the earth." (12/4/33 (by Orde) F 7824/128/23, CAB 24/248; 12/1/33 (by Pratt) F 7818/5189/61, CAB 24/28). It may be said that the tendency of the Far East Department at this time was to place China at the center of British Far Eastern policy.

Hence Treasury and the Foreign Office appeared to be divided on the question of concert with Japan. As long as no agreement could be reached, cabinet deliberation on an Anglo-Japanese nonaggression pact was cut off. The DRC report was turned over to the Ministerial Subcommittee on Disarmament. In the process of its investigation, Chamberlain objected to the DRC's priorities for the stationing of forces. He advocated a defense policy designed to withstand the German threat. Accordingly, he proposed a plan to build up the air force while curbing any increase in the army and navy budgets. He likewise opposed a plan to dispatch the fleet to Singapore, to avoid a display of aggressive intentions toward Japan.

Thus between May and July of 1934, a heated national defense debate developed between two groups within the government. Chamberlain of the Treasury faction sought to reduce military expenditures in deference to domestic economic recovery and social reform. The Imperial faction, together with the navy, took the defense of the empire seriously, emphasizing the need to expand naval power. The foreign policy discussion over the improvement of relations with Japan was naturally intertwined with this debate (Endicott, 1975: 62-72; Trotter, 1975: 82-92).

The Ripples of The Hirota Statement

When Sir Robert Clive took up his post as British Ambassador to Japan, he was ignorant of the debate which the question of an Anglo-Japanese nonaggression pact had evoked at the highest levels of his government. When he had his second meeting with Foreign Minister Kōki Hirota on July 3, 1934, Hirota told him, "Japan would be ready to conclude nonaggression pacts with America and Great Britain." The uninformed Clive misconstrued this announcement as a passing whim. He accorded it so little significance that he relayed it to London by sea mail. Moreover, Clive's communiqué reported merely that Hirota was "convinced that the old spirit of the Anglo-Japanese alliance remained" and that "the Emperor was most emphatic in his desire for the friendliest relations with Great Britain" (Harada, 1951: 230-232).

Clive's communication reached London on August 7 and stirred sizable ripples within the government. Hirota's appointment as Foreign Minister the previous autumn had been viewed favorably in England. Sir Francis Lindley, Clive's predecessor as ambassador to Tokyo, had delivered a message from Foreign Secretary Simon on December 26 expressing hope for amity between the two nations and a restoration of the goodwill which had characterized the Anglo-Japanese Alliance (Harada, 1951: 230-232). In his reply, Hirota had displayed a conciliatory posture. He lamented the termination of the Alliance as "a disastrous blunder." Both nations, he said, should act "in the spirit of that Alliance" (Trotter, 1975: 39-40). This expression of friendship had raised high expectations on the part of the pro-Japan faction of Chamberlain and Fisher concerning Hirota's policy. Clive's report could not help but swell their hopes for the conclusion of a nonaggression pact.

The word from Clive reverberated throughout the Foreign Office as well. Vacationing Foreign Secretary Simon responded in an August 20 note to the undersecretary, in which he spoke very positively about a nonaggression pact. Simon pointed out that such an arrangement would be an effective device to moderate Japanese naval expansion. He also suggested that Japan would seek some reciprocal move such as British recognition of Manchukuo (DBFP: 15-16). Within the Foreign Office, Sir Robert Craigie, head of the American Department, shared the Foreign Secretary's optimism. Craigie, who closely reflected the Chamberlain-Fisher line, believed that Hirota intended to use the pact to counter the Japanese Navy's obstinacy on disarmament. He expressed on August 22 his opinion that Hirota's advance "merits sympathetic consideration here" (DBFP: 17-18). The negativism of the Far East Department, and that of Undersecretary Vansittart, was as strong at this time as it had been the previous March. In an August 28 memorandum, Far East Department chief Charles Orde asserted that "a nonaggression pact might give [Japan] added confidence in her expansionist tendencies and hamper us in resisting them" (DBFP: 19-20).

In the cabinet, Simon, who represented the Liberal Party, had a weak political base. He also displayed a lack of firm judgment in foreign affairs. Anxiety and confusion tended to mar his diplomatic leadership. Accordingly, his advocacy of an Anglo-Japanese nonaggression pact lacked strong support and vacillated when he faced resistance from subordinates. And thus, it was necessary for him to have strong support from Chamberlain in moving forward. On September 1, the vacationing Chancellor of Exchequer sent Simon a letter enclosing a long memorandum for cabinet discussion. The letter admonished the Foreign Secretary that "this is one of those critical points in history which test the statesman's capacity and foresight. . . . I hope you may think sufficiently well of the idea to pursue it and that you will someday be remembered as the author of the Simon-Hirota pact." Thus did Chamberlain try to stir Simon to action (DBFP: 24-25).

The lengthy memorandum enclosed in the letter to Simon delineated, in sixteen points, Chamberlain's argument for the conclusion of an Anglo-Japanese nonaggression pact. This document repeated the same line of reasoning he had advanced in the cabinet. However, two points are noteworthy. Point four touched upon Manchukuo, saying that so long as the Open Door was respected, Manchukuo represented an opportunity for British exporters. The fifth point posited the recent disclosure that in June Japan had approached America on a nonaggression pact as evidence that Japan was willing to discuss the conditions for such an agreement with Britain. The Chamberlain memorandum concluded that Japan indeed desired a nonaggression pact and that negotiations with the Japanese government on the particulars of an agreement should begin at once (DBFP: 25-31).

As expected, the Far East Department of the Foreign Office strongly resisted Chamberlain's proposal. Orde, in a memorandum of September 4, argued that the conclusion of an Anglo-Japanese pact was fraught with the danger of inducing a Japanese attack against the Soviet Union (DBFP: 31-34). Simon's position again wavered before hostile voices within the Foreign Office (9/7/34, FO 371/181 77/9921). The Foreign Secretary was caught in the middle between soft and hardline positions. While pressing

Japan to pay the price of restraining its actions in China, he posed an alternative basically along the lines of appeasement (see also Chamberlain to Simon on Sept. 10, 1934, in DBFP: 40-41).

On September 25, the British government consented to the opening of "strictly unofficial" ambassadorial talks with Japan on a nonaggression pact (DBFP: 41-42). Accordingly, Simon instructed Clive to ascertain Japan's view on two questions: (1) What was the intent of Hirota's July 3 statement? (2) Could Britain obtain, along with a pact, satisfactory guarantees of Japanese restraint in China? (Trotter, 1975: 101; DBFP: 41-42).

What indeed was the true meaning of the Hirota statement on an Anglo-Japanese nonaggression pact? Unfortunately there is no Japanese record of the content of the July 3 Hirota-Clive conversations. Nonetheless, the clear commitment of Hirota at this time to the improvement of relations with Great Britain and the United States makes it quite conceivable that a positive statement was made. As for relations with the United States, Ambassador Hiroshi Saitō and Secretary of State Cordell Hull met twice in May to discuss a Japanese-American "joint declaration" whose focal point would be a mutual commitment to stabilize power in the Pacific. It was rumored that Hirota desired to meet with President Roosevelt in Honolulu to discuss the matter (Clive to Simon, 7/5/34, F 4798/373/23, FO 410/95/ 9771).[4]

It can be surmised that the Japanese Foreign Minister's plans to pursue a parallel approach in relations with Britain lay behind the July 3 Hirota statement. In this regard, the arguments of Shigenori Tōgō, chief of the Foreign Ministry's Euro-American Section, are particularly relevant. In a lengthy memorandum of April, 1933, Tōgō dealt with the direction Japanese foreign policy should take in the face of the international isolation provoked by Japan's withdrawal from the League of Nations. In this document, Tōgō stated that "in China, Japan and Britain have

4. Memoranda by Hull, May 1934, in U.S. Department of State *Foreign Relations of the United States* I (1934: 650-661). Hereafter, this volume will be referred to in the text as simply *FRUS*.

significant shared interests. With England we have more grounds for cooperation than with any other nation. It is essential to promote cordial relations and to work toward concerted action with Great Britain" (Tōgō, 1952: 85).

It is also appropriate to recall that cooperation with the British represented longstanding diplomatic orthodoxy in the tradition of Kasumigaseki. Besides, the Imperial Army leadership frequently promoted the option of a concert line with Britain.[5] At this time, the diplomatic views of War Minister Sadao Araki, who took friendship with England seriously, were known in London (Snow to Orde, 12/22/33, F 591/591/23, CAB 21/1007/9669). Needless to say, feelings of affection for Britain were strong among the emperor and such court intimates as Nobuaki Makino. The emperor's cordial aspirations with regard to England were occasionally reported to the British government through diplomatic channels and served to encourage the pro-Japan faction.

The search for the true meaning of the Hirota statement inevitably encounters the domestic debate over naval disarmament. The Japanese government had nearly taken the final steps to firm its policy on equalization of the naval arms ratio with Britain and the United States and the renunciation of the Washington disarmament treaty. Nonetheless, there remained disagreements between the government and the military. Though a decision to abandon the treaty and secure parity had been reached in the navy under the dominance of the "fleet faction," some naval officials were still reluctant. The War Ministry, concerned about the allocation of the budget, was opposed (Japanese Defense Agency, War History Office, 1975: 280). The Foreign Ministry leadership, especially influential bureau chief Tōgō, was unalterably antagonistic toward the Naval Ministry's proposed

---

5. Kasumigaseki is the "Foggy Bottom" of Tokyo. The term denotes mainstream Japanese diplomacy. In the latter half of the 1920s, War Minister Kazushige Ugaki and his cohorts advocated rapprochement with Britain as a countermove against Chinese nationalism and Bolshevism. Moreover, in its orientation favoring such rapprochement, Tanaka diplomacy diverged from Shidehara diplomacy. On this subject, see Hosoya (1978).

"common maximum" armament plan, and exchanged heated words on the subject with Military Affairs Bureau chief Zengo Yoshida (Tōgō, 1952: 92-93).

The new cabinet of Keisuke Okada which took office July 7 had similar difficulty reaching agreement on naval disarmament. In the Five-Minister Conference which met twice that month, Hirota and the Prime Minister joined hands to counter the hardline position of Navy Minister Mineo Ōsumi. They advocated avoiding a rupture of the upcoming London Naval Conference and sought to alter the navy's position through a plan for the gradual implementation of an equal ratio (Gaimushō hyakunenshi hensan iinkai, 1969: 516-618; Japanese Defense Agency, War History Office, 1975: 281). Was the proposal for an Anglo-Japanese nonaggression pact used by Hirota as a tactic to deal with navy hardliners? Craigie of the Foreign Office understood Hirota's scheme to be just that.

Despite resistance by Hirota and the Foreign Ministry, the fleet faction of Kanji Katō, Nobumasa Suetsugu, and other intractables had its way. The cabinet on September 7 decided the government's final policy for the London Naval Conference. Japan committed itself to abandoning the Washington treaty and concluding a disarmament agreement based on the principle of "common maximum armament." From this time on, the Anglo-Japanese nonaggression pact, from Hirota's standpoint, was bereft of meaning.

The Federation of British Industries Mission

On September 27, 1934, a delegation of the Federation of British Industries (FBI) arrived in Japan. This event seemed to follow on the heels of the instructions to Ambassador Clive to sound out the position of the Japanese government on an Anglo-Japanese nonaggression pact. The entourage was headed by the Federation's past president Lord Barnby. With him came Federation board chairman Guy Locock; Julian Piggott, representing the Iron and Steel Federation; and banker Charles Seligman, director of Seligman Brothers. Their ostensible purpose was to investigate the situation in Manchukuo and explore possibilities for investing in the Manchurian market and expanding the export of British heavy industrial products. It was not a government mission, but in composition and size it was the most significant delegation to visit Manchuria since the Lytton Commission. Understandably, it was widely construed as an indication of a shift in British policy toward Manchuria.

A political task beyond the designing of an economic thrust into the Manchurian market is quite evident in the circumstances surrounding the dispatch of the mission. The man responsible for behind-the-scenes maneuvers was A.H.F. Edwardes, former agent of the Chinese maritime customs and at the time a financial advisor to the Manchukuo government. Later he would become a consultant to the Japanese embassy in London. He was close to Treasury Undersecretary Fisher and a driving force behind the Chamberlain-Fisher line. Confident of Anglo-Japanese political rapprochement, Edwardes made the FBI Mission an important step in a shift of British policy toward recognition of Manchukuo (Endicott, 1975: 74-77; Trotter, 1975: 115-131; Kihata, 1934: 20-22). Since May, the scheme spearheaded by Edwardes and Fisher had acquired the backing of steel and machinery exporters interested in the Manchurian market. It had also gained the support of *Morning Post* editor-in-chief H. A. Gwynne and the cooperation of the pro-Japan faction (Cable 275, 5/26/34).[6] What is especially noteworthy is a cable reporting the favorable posture of King George V (Cable 1005, 10/5/34) and the enthusiasm of the Prince of Wales who had made "suggestions" regarding the composition of the delegation (Cable 380, 7/12/34). Apparently the Chamberlain-Fisher line had achieved broad support among conservatives.

Tokyo first got wind of the mission from Japan's ambassador to London, Tsuneo Matsudaira. In late May, Matsudaira sent a report entitled "The Recognition of Manchukuo" in which he noted that the FBI project was under consideration (Cable 275,

6. Until otherwise noted, this and the following cables and memoranda are recorded in the Foreign Ministry Records.

5/26/34). A July 12 Cable (380) reported the selection of the participants. It also stated that, though the mission was sent nominally for business purposes, its real aim was to promote British friendship with Japan and Manchukuo. Then, in an August 29 private message to Foreign Minister Hirota, Matsudaira elaborated upon the motives behind the scheme:

> Since the end of last year those Britons who are concerned about Anglo-Japanese friendship and the recognition of Manchukuo have been meeting from time to time. They have seen to it that Britain be the first to send a delegation of the calibre of the FBI Mission to explore means to promote understanding between Britain and Japan. It seems to me that upon their return to England they will influence public opinion for the recognition of Manchukuo.

Matsudaira went on to call the foreign minister's attention to the efforts of Fisher, the pivotal role of the prince in the selection of the head of the delegation, and the king's intense interest in the project. Finally he urged Hirota to accord the mission full hospitality.

Japanese domestic opinion viewed the FBI Mission as an instrument of rapprochement with Great Britain. The Tokyo *Nichi Nichi* (October 4, 1934) displayed its favor in an editorial which quoted a statement by Lord Barnby in Japan:

> Nearly all informed people in England today want to see the revival of the Anglo-Japanese Alliance. Until recently there has been hesitancy for fear of offending the United States, but today the situation has changed. It is the hope of the British people to establish a friendly alliance which posits no third party as an enemy. If a like sentiment prevails in Japan, the re-establishment of an alliance will be easier than expected.

About the same time Masanori Itō (1934) published an article in *Kaizō,* "The Rising Argument Favoring an Anglo-Japanese Alliance," in which he stated his anticipation of an agreement with Great Britain which would end Japan's international isolation.

It is noteworthy that within the International Trade Bureau of the Foreign Ministry, the feeling existed that Japan should welcome the FBI Mission, open the Manchurian market to increased British economic penetration, and promote cooperation with all nations. One memorandum reasoned that "if friendly understanding of Japan's Manchuria and China policies can be created we will see the breakdown of the powers' common hostility toward Japan." Chinese officials would terminate their discrimination against Japanese products. As a result, "Japanese exports to China will rise and disputes with Britain in other international markets will subside." It is evident that these officials envisioned an Anglo-Japanese agreement as an effective mechanism to solve Japan's foreign trade difficulties.[7]

Edwardes, who accompanied the FBI Mission, came ready to propose concrete steps for achieving friendly understanding with Japan on the Manchurian market and recognition of Manchukuo. He received secret instructions from Chamberlain and Fisher which he vigorously pursued in meetings with Hirota, Foreign Vice-Minister Mamoru Shigemitsu, Navy Minister Mineo Ōsumi, Army Minister Senjūrō Hayashi, former Army Minister Sadao Araki, and other officials (Endicott, 1975: 74-77). In these talks, Edwardes made specific proposals on Anglo-Japanese cooperation in the Manchurian market: that Britain supply the rolling stock for Manchurian railroads; that British industry participate in the construction of the harbor at Jinwandao; and that Britain finance the loans for these projects (Cable 1005, 10/5/34). These propositions were products of investigations by the pro-Japan faction in London and indicate the interest of British industrial and financial circles in the Manchurian market.

In Tokyo, the Foreign Ministry showed a favorable response to these schemes. However, the army was not prepared to sanction any commitment on railroads and harbors which were already

7. This memorandum, preserved in the Japanese Foreign Ministry Archives (1934a), was composed by Deputy Chief of the Second Division of International Trade, Shikao Matsushima, "Manshū shisatsu Eikoku jitsugyōdan no tōrai ni sai shi waga tsūshō gaikō ni taisuru shinkōsaku no hitsuyō" ("The need for a fresh approach in Japan's trade diplomacy on the occasion of the arrival of the British industrialist party inspecting Manchuria").

under the management of the South Manchurian Railway (Cable 1015, 10/8/34). In the end the outcome of talks between Manchukuo officials and the FBI Mission was expressed in a vaguely worded joint statement on October 13. It read, in part, "There is no objection to the principle that British industry cooperate in the development of Manchuria. . . . Concrete measures are now under consideration by the Manchukuo government."[8]

This accord was announced so that the mission would not have to go home empty-handed, and from the start there was virtually no possibility of reaching more definite terms. The army, which controlled Manchuria, was negatively disposed toward the participation of foreign enterprise in Manchurian development. It adhered to the basic position that Japanese products should monopolize the Manchurian market.

Following its return to England in December, the FBI Mission released its report to the public. That statement related the mission's favorable impression of economic development in Japan and Manchuria. It optimistically proclaimed bright prospects for the export of English capital for the rapidly developing Manchurian market. But since Japan's Manchurian policy was controlled by the army, the report offered British economic circles a vain illusion.

Before the publication of the report Locock wrote a letter dated December 10 to Sir Horace Wilson (12/10/34, CP 9 (34), CAB 24/253), chief industrial advisor to the government. This letter bears upon the FBI Mission's political purpose "the promotion of Anglo-Japanese friendship." It stressed the need for the establishment of political understanding between Britain and Japan: "The solution of our trade difficulties with Japan and the extent to which British industry will be given opportunities to participate in the development of Manchukuo will depend very largely upon whether the political relations between Japan and Great Britain can be placed upon a basis of friendly cooperation." This communication was presented at a cabinet meeting the following

8. This is a translation of the record of a conference between the Manchukuo government and the British inspection party, October 13, 1934.

January and was used as a basis for rationalizing the Chamberlain-Fisher policy of rapprochement with Japan.[9] It also reveals the domestic political aim accorded to the FBI Mission.

The American Reaction to
Anglo-Japanese Rapprochement

A dinner reception was given for the FBI Mission in Tokyo on September 28. Acting in accordance with instructions from London, Ambassador Clive took the occasion to extend his first query to Foreign Minister Hirota concerning the intent of the "Hirota statement." In a communiqué to London (DBFP: 51-53), the Ambassador described Hirota's response:

> Japanese Government were very anxious in case Naval Conference failed that there should be no break in friendly relations with Great Britain and he would like to see some more definite understanding. This might perhaps take the form of a non-aggression pact.

This word from Hirota was too obscure to clarify the concrete details of the pact. Indeed, it showed a lack of enthusiasm.

The next British approach was made by Foreign Secretary Simon to Ambassador Matsudaira in London on October 8. Simon asked whether Hirota had "any kind of definite idea" concerning a nonaggression pact. Simon went on to declare that

> the Manchurian issue is now a thing of the past. Personally I have not the least appetite for retracing the arguments of the past. Rather, what is of present importance to us is some kind of guarantee for the interests of Britain in China outside Manchuria.

Thus, the foreign secretary underscored the necessity for Anglo-Japanese understanding on China proper, south of the Great

9. At a January 1935 Cabinet meeting, the Chamberlain-Fisher group presented the FBI Mission report. The Far East Department of the Foreign Office responded to this in a memorandum by George Sansom. On this, see Trotter (1975: 122-131) and Kihata (1977: 21-22).

Wall.[10] In this Matsudaira concurred and expressed his hope that Anglo-Japanese understanding on China would be reached, but the ambassador declined to reveal any particulars on a non-aggression pact. He even mentioned that a special envoy was expected to arrive shortly from Tokyo with instructions on the matter (DBFP: 51-53).

At the time, progress was being made in reconciling the Chamberlain-Fisher position and that of the Far East Department of the Foreign Office toward the "Chamberlain memorandum" of September 1. The outcome was the drafting of a new document, a Chamberlain-Simon joint memorandum entitled "The Future of Anglo-Japanese Relations." The October 16 joint statement, while based on the original Chamberlain note, incorporated the views of the Foreign Office. It advocated the conclusion of an Anglo-Japanese nonaggression pact, but also listed three significant needs which show Chamberlain's concessions to the Foreign Office:

(1) to obtain a Japanese guarantee of the territorial integrity of China proper, south of the Great Wall;
(2) to explore with the United States the establishment of a tripartite Anglo-Japanese-American nonaggression pact;
(3) to use pact negotiations with Japan *as a lever* to soften Japan's demands at the disarmament conference.

At a meeting of the cabinet on October 24, the Chamberlain-Simon joint memorandum was introduced but shelved for a lack of basic information on the Japanese position (DBFP: 61-65).

To Foreign Minister Hirota, the September 7 decision by the Japanese cabinet adopting a hardline policy for the disarmament conference obviated an important rationale for an Anglo-Japanese nonaggression pact. The time was past when the pact could serve as a means to counter the navy's strong demands. Hirota's statement of September 28 to Clive can be viewed as a reflection of this development. Top officials in the Foreign Ministry met and studied the issue of the pact after receiving Matsudaira's report of October 9. The record of Vice-Minister

10. Unless otherwise noted, this and the following cables and memoranda are preserved in the Japanese Foreign Ministry Archives (1935).

Shigemitsu's oral presentation of October 20 reflects the "united thinking" of the Ministry:

It is useless to discuss or establish a nonaggression pact which deals with the issue of guarantees or the problem of securing the interests of the various nations in China. The pact will not serve to achieve Japan's demands with regard to disarmament.

This conclusion, by warning against a repetition of the mistakes of the Washington Conference, amounted to a rejection of the nonaggression pact. By this time, the "realization of Japan's position on disarmament" had become a matter of supreme importance. Shigemitsu continued,

On the one hand it is appropriate to conduct bilateral discussions with Britain and the United States for the purpose of promoting friendly relations with them. But it would not be in the interest of Japanese relations with the United States and other powers to discuss with the British government at this time the problem of securing interests in China.[11]

It is evident here that relations with the United States were being taken into account.

Insofar as this document goes, it can be assumed that Edwardes, under orders from Chamberlain and Fisher, was totally ineffective in his efforts vis-à-vis Japan. It can also be said that the intentions of the pro-Japan faction were inadequately communicated to the Japanese Foreign Ministry leadership.

The Japanese government's official response to the British feelers on a nonaggression pact is given in an October 29 cable from Hirota to Matsudaira. This statement accepts the conclusions of the aforementioned meeting of the Foreign Ministry officials. As for the real meaning of the previous "Hirota statement," the message (Cable 309, 10/29/34) explained,

11. This memorandum, "Honshō kanbu kaigi no itchi seru ikō narabini daijin no iken omo sanshaku no ue shūkankyokuka ni okeru kunrei ritsuanjō no sankō ni shisuru mokuteki o motte jikan no kōjutsu seraretaru mono nari" ("Vice-minister's dictation for the purpose of drafting instructions by relevant bureaus, taking the positions of the foreign minister and staff meeting into consideration") and dated October 20, 1934, is kept in the Japanese Foreign Ministry Archives (1934b).

> The other day I spoke to the British ambassador as follows: The success of the disarmament conference can be expected only when the three major participants—Japan, Britain, and the United States—share a mutual understanding and good faith that will disallow aggression. So I proposed, as one possible means, the extension of the Four-power Pact.

In short, the message made no mention at all of a nonaggression pact. Moreover, Hirota reiterated his concern that Matsudaira, in discussions concerning the furtherance of Anglo-Japanese friendship, "take care not to make any commitment which would circumscribe Japan's future position in East Asia." He thoroughly warned the ambassador to "especially take care not to raise American suspicion that Japan is conducting under-the-table political dealings with Great Britain."

Bilateral negotiations at preliminary sessions of the London Naval Conference had begun October 23 and were now in progress. On October 30, Foreign Secretary Simon, seeking to avoid the breakup of the parlay, submitted to Matsudaira a compromise formula which he called his private proposal (Cable 512, 10/31/34). The basic elements of this formula were:

(1) consideration for Japan's need to preserve "prestige." For instance, Japan might save face by a conference declaration accepting the right to equality in armaments;

(2) a secret, trilateral "gentlemen's agreement" on naval construction, for a specified time, to prevent a naval arms race;

(3) the conclusion of an Anglo-American-Japanese nonaggression pact which would afford Japan a sense of security. However, Japan would have to reject territorial aggression in China.

The American government was very uneasy over British moves at this time. It was concerned about the FBI Mission and the British decision to initiate its own approach to Japan on naval disarmament, a move incompatible with the American preference for a joint Anglo-American front against Japan. During October and November, reports of Anglo-Japanese rapprochement and discussion of a nonaggression pact rippled through the American news media.[12] How did Washington leaders view British moves on disarmament? To them, the British appeared to be pursuing separate negotiations with the Japanese. The British had chosen not to join the United States in adamantly opposing Japan's demand for parity. Rather, they sought to play the role of mediator in the face of Japanese-American animosity. Furthermore, American leaders saw the British as ready to accept the Manchurian situation as a fait accompli and to work out a political accommodation with the Japanese on China.[13]

Little by little, the feeling spread among American officials that they must strike a blow against Britain's political dealing with Japan. On November 6, Norman H. Davis, head of the American delegation to the naval conference, sent a report to President Roosevelt. This message pointed out to the President the existence of a deeply rooted pro-Japanese movement within the British government whose participants were distrustful of the United States and opposed to dealing with Washington. Nonetheless, the delegation expected that so long as the Western powers did not act in a high-handed fashion, Japan would eventually be restored to a sound attitude in foreign affairs (in Nixon,1969: 258-261). Roosevelt was adamantly opposed to the British moves of rapprochement with Japan. In a cable to Davis on November 9 he suggested the possibility of a pressure tactic, the use of the British dominions as intermediaries:

> Simon and a few other Tories must be constantly impressed with the simple fact that if Great Britain is even suspected of preferring to play with Japan to playing with us, I shall be compelled, in the interest of American security, to approach public sentiment in Canada, Australia, New Zealand and South Africa in a definite effort to make these Dominions understand clearly that their

12. Reports that Japan and Britain were involved in secret negotiations over a nonaggression pact proposed by Japan and appeared in the American press several weeks before (*DBFP:* 82).

13. For example, at a September 26 joint State Department-Department of Navy meeting, Undersecretary of State William Phillips warned that signs of "diplomatic dealing" between Japan and Britain indicated British consideration of policies to justify Japanese aggression in Manchuria. See the memorandum by P. Moffat of September 26, 1934: Roosevelt Papers (Hyde Park), file Japan 1934 (2).

future security is linked with us in the United States [in Nixon: 1969: 263-264].

As if echoing the mind of Washington, a "pro-American faction" suddenly made itself heard in the British press in mid-November. Including such figures as General Jan C. Smuts and Lord Lothian, the group concentrated its efforts upon British government leaders. They intoned the unity of "English-speaking peoples" and argued that a close American connection was the traditional foundation of England's foreign policy. Commensurately, the pro-Americans called for maintaining a strategy of Anglo-American cooperation on disarmament. They heaped criticism on "the pro-Japanese and anti-American element" which they found "all over the place, like a snake in the grass" (Watt, 1965: 95-98; Pelz, 1974: 141-143). The arguments of General Smuts, the South African veteran statesman, seemed to represent the voice of all the dominions.

Thus the Anglo-Japanese nonaggression pact did not materialize. The course of domestic and international developments, and the American hardline attitude in particular, had a restraining effect upon the MacDonald cabinet which had put off deliberation of the Chamberlain-Simon joint memorandum. These circumstances strengthened the position of those, including the prime minister, who counselled caution.

Beyond this, however, an instruction sent from Tokyo had a decisive effect on British loss of enthusiasm for a nonaggression pact. At a meeting with Foreign Secretary Simon on November 19, Ambassador Matsudaira presented for the first time the official Japanese position on the pact:

> Foreign Minister Hirota thinks that an arrangement like a trilateral nonaggression pact is not necessarily the best course to take. It would be preferable to simply renew and extend the Four-Power Pact, which represents the same spirit [Cable 532, 11/21/34].

At the same time, Matsudaira apologized for having misrepresented Ambassador Shigeru Yoshida, who had arrived in England ten days earlier, as a "special envoy." Yoshida's task, he asserted, was no more than that of an inspector.

One could imagine the deep disappointment of Chamberlain, who since March had championed in the cabinet the idea of an Anglo-Japanese nonaggression pact and who had put stock in the July "Hirota statement." On November 21, American envoy Davis cabled Washington that

> Neville Chamberlain . . . has come to the conclusion that Great Britain should make no agreement with Japan to which the United States is not a party, that Anglo-American cooperation is a vital necessity to world peace and stability [FRUS I: 358-359].

Again, in a letter to Roosevelt on November 27:

> The small willful group that favored playing with Japan, and who were supported by commercial interests seeking trade advantages, have apparently been losing ground. . . . Chamberlain told Lord Lothian that he was now convinced Japan could not be trusted. . . . He thought, however, that it was better to avoid a rupture just now for fear that we would drive Japan in desperation to make an alliance with Germany [in Nixon, 1969: 290-293].

Thus the curtain closed upon the drama of Anglo-Japanese rapprochement which revolved around the saga of an Anglo-Japanese nonaggression pact from the spring through the fall of 1934. The following year, actors in new attire would go onstage in a new scene, the Leith Ross Mission. Again, the one who would rotate the stage on the British side would be Sir Warren Fisher.

Conclusion

In the end, the scheme of an Anglo-Japanese nonaggression pact did not bear fruit. The fears of Chamberlain and others who advocated concert with Japan materialized, and Japan little by little turned to Germany as an alliance partner. The idea that a German connection was needed to prepare for a confrontation with the Soviet Union gripped the middle level officers of the

Army General Staff. Secret, persistent negotiations by Military Attaché Hiroshi Oshima in Berlin led by the end of 1935 to the opening of discussions on a Japanese-German anti-Comintern pact. With the conclusion in November 1936 of the Anti-Comintern Pact, the tilt of Japanese diplomacy toward Germany became a certainty.

In this era of Japanese diplomacy in search of concert, was the option of Great Britain as a concert partner an impossibility? Had the Anglo-Japanese nonaggression pact retained the character originally conceived by Chamberlain (a means to reduce the budget, allow an emphasis on European defense, and lessen economic friction with Japan), there would have been considerable room for Japan to respond and for discussion to proceed along a "Japanese appeasement" line. Circumstances on the Japanese side were favorable. Not only were there pro-British forces in the court circles and the business community, but even some army leaders stood as spokesmen for the utility of a British concert as the best counterweight to the Soviet threat. Moreover, the traditional pro-British bent of the Foreign Ministry remained strong.

Nonetheless, strong argument from the Foreign Office forced Chamberlain to add to his original scheme a new condition: a guarantee of Japanese nonaggression in China. This ran fundamentally counter to the China policy of the Japanese army and was unacceptable to the Foreign Ministry mainstream as well. Consequently, room for compromise was significantly narrowed. Furthermore, the issue of the pact became intertwined with the naval disarmament talks. When the pact took on the character of a mechanism to restrain Japan's demand for parity, it ran into a head-on collision with the mainstream position in the Japanese navy which assigned highest priority to the achievement of an equal ratio.

Chamberlain was one of the most powerful politicians in the Conservative Party, while Fisher had considerable influence among high officials through widespread powers of appointment. These two were the driving force behind the policy of cooperation with Japan. But so long as the Chamberlain-Fisher line excluded

Foreign Secretary Simon, it lacked the means to translate itself into foreign policy. The Foreign Office's Far East Department, with a direct channel to Simon, urged revision of the Chamberlain-Fisher line. As a result, the compromise produced between Treasury and the Foreign Office significantly narrowed Japan's options. American pressure, exerted directly upon Prime Minister MacDonald and other cabinet members through Foreign Office and other channels must be taken into account as a factor acting against the establishment of an Anglo-Japanese nonaggression pact.

When these factors are fully examined, one may conclude that the objective conditions for the creation of an Anglo-Japanese nonaggression pact were nearly all absent at the time. Nonetheless, the events of 1934 cannot be brushed aside as a mere episode in the history of Anglo-Japanese relations. The question of the pact bears historical significance and demands the attention of those who would comprehend Far Eastern international politics in the mid-1930s.

Date of receipt of final manuscript: May 30, 1981

REFERENCES

ENDICOTT, S. L. (1975) Diplomacy and Enterprise. British China Policy 1933-1937. Manchester, England: Manchester Univ. Press.

Federation of British Industries (1934) Report of the Mission to the Far East, August to November 1934. London: Author.

FEILING, K. (1946) The Life of Neville Chamberlain. London: Macmillan.

Gaimushō hyakunenshi hensan iinkai (1969) Gaimushō no hyakunen (The Centennial History of the Japanese Ministry of Foreign Affairs), Volume II. Tokyo: Hara Shobō.

HARADA, K. (1951) Saionji kō to seikyoku. Tokyo: Iwanami Shoten.

HOSOYA, C. (1978) Washinton taisei no tokushitsu to henyō (The characteristics and transformation of the Washington order), pp. 3-40 in C. Hosoya and M. Saitō (eds.) Washinton taisei to Nichibei kankei (The Washington Order and Japanese-American Relations). Tokyo: Tokyō Daigaku Shuppankai.

ITŌ, M. (1934) "Nichiei dōmei ron no taitō" ("The rising argument favoring an Anglo-Japanese alliance"). Kaizō: February.

Japanese Defense Agency, War History Office (1975) Daihonei kaigunbu: rengō kantai. (General Staff Office: Joint Fleet). Volume I. Tokyo: Asagumo Shimbumsha.

Japanese Foreign Ministry Archives (1935) File "1935 nen kaisai no kaigun gunshuku kaigi ikken, yobi kōshō kankei" ("Materials on the preliminary negotiations of the naval disarmament conference of 1935").

————— (1934a) File "Eikoku jitsugyōka Nichiman shisatsudan kankei" ("Materials related to the British industrialist inspection tour of Japan and Manchuria").

————— (1934b) File "Teikoku no taishi seisaku kankei" ("Materials on Japan's China policy").

KIHATA, Y. (1977) "Nitchū sensō zenshi ni okeru kokusai kankyō: Igirisu no tainichi seisaku, 1934" ("The international environment of the Sino-Japanese War: British policy toward Japan, 1934"). Kyōyō gakka kiyō (The Proceedings of the Department of Social Sciences, College of General Education, University of Tokyō) 9: 1-26.

MEDLICOTT, W. N., D. DAKIN, and M. E. LAMBERT [eds.] (1973) Documents on British Foreign Policy. Series 2, Volume 13. London: HMSO.

NIXON, E. B. (1969) Franklin D. Roosevelt and Foreign Affairs, 1933-1937. Volume II. Cambridge, MA: Belknap Press.

PELZ, S. E. (1974) Race to Pearl Harbor. Cambridge, MA: Harvard Univ. Press.

TŌGŌ, S. (1952) Jidai no ichimen. Tokyo. (Translated by F. Tōgō and B. B. Blakeney, The Cause of Japan. New York: Simon and Schuster, 1956).

TROTTER, A. (1975) Britain and East Asia, 1933-1937. London: Cambridge Univ. Press.

————— (1974) "Tentative steps for an Anglo-Japanese rapprochement in 1934." Modern Asian Studies 8: 59-83.

United States Dept. of State (1934) Foreign Relations of the United States. Volume I. Washington, DC: Government Printing Office.

WATT, D. C. (1965) Personalities and Policies. London: Longmans.

ERRATA

In Christopher Chase-Dunn's article, "Interstate System and Capitalist World-Economy: One Logic or Two?" (*ISQ*, 25(1), March, 1981), errors of hyphenation were made in the production stage. These errors altered the meaning of some important concepts in Chase-Dunn's argument. Throughout the article, "world-empire" and "world-economy" should have been hyphenated, whereas on page 33 there should be no hyphen in the phrase "single commodity economy." We apologize for the error.

Contributors

RUTH W. ARAD is a lecturer in the Faculty of Management at Tel Aviv University. She has published articles in many journals including *Journal of International Economics, International Economic Review,* and *Weltwirtschaftliches Archiv.* She is also a co-author of *Sharing Global Resources,* published as part of the 1980s project of the U.S. Council of Foreign Relations.

JAMES A. CAPORASO is currently Andrew Mellon Professor of International Studies at the Graduate School of International Studies of the University of Denver. He is the guest editor of a special issue of *International Organization* on dependence and dependency in the global system, as well as author of articles in *International Studies Quarterly* and *Journal of European Integration.* His recent work focuses on the processes of economic growth and development in the periphery and the effect of such processes on advanced capitalist countries.

SEEV HIRSCH is the Mel and Sheila Jaffee Professor of International Trade at the Faculty of Management, Tel Aviv University. He has published a number of books, including *Location of Industry and International Competitiveness,* and *Rich Man's, Poor Man's and Every Man's Goods—Aspects of Industrialization.* His articles have been published in several journals, including *Oxford Economic Papers, Weltwirtschaftliches Archiv,* and *World Development.*

CHIHIRO HOSOYA is Professor of International Relations at Hitotsubashi University (Tokyo) and President of the Japan Association of International Relations. In addition to Japanese journal publications, he has written an article on Japanese foreign policy decision-making that appeared in *World Politics.* He is also the author of two books dealing with relations between Japan and the early Soviet Union, and has co-authored a four-volume study of relations between Japan and the United States during the decade that preceded Pearl Harbor.

JAMES H. POLHEMUS is Senior Lecturer in the School of Social Sciences, Deakin University, Victoria, Australia. During 1979-1981, he is Senior Lecturer in the Department of Political and Administrative Studies, University College of Botswana, University of Botswana and Swaziland. His publications include articles on the Organization of African Unity and on Nigerian foreign policy.

JOHN E. TURNER is Regents' Professor of Political Science at the University of Minnesota, where he specializes in comparative politics, focusing primarily on sociopolitical change. His authored and co-authored works include *American Government in Comparative Perspective, Labour's Doorstep Politics in London, Political Parties in Action,* and *The Political Basis of Economic Development,* as well as co-authored or co-edited books on the USSR, Japan, and the methodology of comparative research. He has also published a number of journal articles and contributed chapters in the comparative field. He has just completed a collaborative study of community development in Korea.